PATTON AND HIS THIRD ARMY

PATTON AND HIS THIRD ARMY

Gen. Brenton G. Wallace

with an introduction by Martin Blumenson

STACKPOLE
BOOKS

First paperback edition 2000

Published by
STACKPOLE BOOKS
5067 Ritter Road
Mechanicsburg, PA 17055
www.stackpolebooks.com

Printed in the United States of America

10 9 8 7 6 5 4 3 2

Front cover photograph courtesy of the U. S. Army Military History Institute

Cover design by Wendy A. Reynolds

Library of Congress Cataloging-in-Publication Data

Wallace, Brenton Greene, 1891–
    Patton and his Third Army / Brenton G. Wallace ; with an introduction by Martin Blumenson.
        p. cm.
    Originally published: Harrisburg, Pa. : Military Service Pub. Co., c1946.
    ISBN 0-8117-2896-X
    1. World War, 1939–1945—Regimental histories—United States—Army, Third. 2. World War, 1939–1945—Campaigns—Western Europe. 3. Patton, George S. (George Smith) 1885–1945. 4. United States. Army. Army, 3rd. I. Title.

D769.26 3d.W35 2000
940.54'21—dc21
                                                    00-035752

DEDICATION

To our beloved Commander, General George Smith Patton, Jr., and the officers and men of the Third U. S. Army—especially those who did not return.

APPRECIATION

In appreciation of the loyal love, devotion and assistance rendered by my Wife, who, with two sons and a husband serving overseas, was probably the best soldier of the lot.

Her help and encouragement as well as that of our daughter, Dorothy Jane, who did all of the typing in connection with the writing of this book, is greatly appreciated.

TABLE OF CONTENTS

		Page
	Introduction	ix
	Preface	xvi
1	The Two "Greatest Bluffs in History"	1
2	The Preparation and Build Up	5
3	The Staff—Headquarters Third U.S. Army	14
4	Across the Beaches	23
5	The Breakthrough	30
6	Across France—The Bomb Explodes	41
7	The Falaise Pocket	52
8	Paris Falls	64
9	Stopped, But Not by the Germans	78
10	Line of the Moselle	94
11	Capture of the Metz and the Saar Valley	116
12	Battle of the Bulge	137
13	The Eifel Hills to the Rhine: Capture of Coblenz and Saar Basin	165
14	Forcing the Rhine and Across Germany—Entering Czechoslovakia and Austria	180
15	Patton—The Man	196

APPENDICES

I	Chronological Record of Events	215
II	Third Army Units and Commanders	221
III	The Bastogne Surrender Ultimatum and Reply	223
IV	A Typical Casualty Report from the Third Army	224
V	General Order No. 1, 1 January 1945	228
VI	Commendation, 26 January 1945	230
VII	The Christmas Message and Prayer Sent the Third Army, 1944	231

TABLE OF CONTENTS
MAPS

Page

Operation COBRA—The Breakthrough 31

The Bomb Explodes 43

The Falaise Pocket 53

Paris Falls 66

Paris Past the Moselle 79

The Line of the Moselle 96

Capture of Metz and the Saar Valley 123

The Battle of the Bulge 143

Eifel Hills to the Rhine 169

Across the Rhine to Victory 187

From England to Victory 232

Introduction

FOUR months after World War II ended in Europe, Brenton G. Wallace, newly promoted to brigadier general, returned from Germany to his home in the Philadelphia area. He had, no doubt, already started work on his narrative, though maybe only in his mind, and before long, he finished his remarkable account. His book, *Patton and His Third Army*, appeared in print in May 1946, exactly a year from V-E day, five months after the death of Gen. George S. Patton, Jr.

As a major publication, Wallace's volume was one of the earliest, perhaps the very first, on the subject, and it prospered. Three additional printings followed rapidly, then a final run in July 1951. All told, seven thousand copies were sold. Spanish and Indian language versions augmented the receipts. In contrast with latter-day figures but in light of experience in those pre-inflationary times fifty-some years ago, the venture was judged to be a decent performance.

An immediate reason for its success was Wallace's particular point of view. Journalists and war correspondents had described the campaigns at great length, but Wallace offered the novel outlook of a participant. As a colonel, he had been a member of the Third Army staff. He had not been in combat, but he had had a responsible managerial position, and his exertions had helped to win victory. He knew the conflict from within the military organization.

What he transmitted in his writing was the excitement of the war. He had celebrated inwardly when he entered towns just liberated. He relished the destruction of enemy weapons and equipment littering the roads. He thrilled to the sight of U.S. soldiers moving forward to the front. He had been elated to drive toward, and, eventually, into the enemy homeland. He had been part of it all, and his place on the team and in the scheme of things made him a savvy observer.

He explained how warfare had been waged. He showed the practice of logistics, the function of artillery, the support of the air forces. He outlined the buildup of American ground forces in the

British Isles before the D-day invasion. He told how prisoners of war were handled and what the food was like. He reproduced a verbatim briefing so that the uninitiated might know and appreciate the rite.

In all, Wallace was charming and clear. He made a great deal of sense about things relatively unknown to civilians and gave his readers valuable insights into the complexities of the war.

He also told about some of his personal adventures, for example, his exchange of conversation with three German prisoners in a camp near Toul, France to get an idea of the enemy state of mind and morale. He passed along the ubiquitous rumors, for instance, the false one of Himmler's taking over from Hitler in November 1944 because Hitler's paranoia supposedly made it impossible for him to govern. He talked of German rockets and jet propelled planes. He discussed the new American proximity fuse on artillery shells. He repeated war stories like seeing French women who were publicly disgraced by having their heads shaved of hair because they had consorted with Germans during the Occupation.

Wallace's prose is instructive and entertaining. Yet in one respect it is disappointing. Wallace wrote his memoir too soon after the war, too quickly after the events. His story on how the campaign unfolded is sometimes off the mark. That came in part from his wartime job.

Assigned to the G-3 or Operations Section, Wallace had been in charge of the liaison officers. They streamed in and out of the Third Army headquarters at all hours of the day and night. Some belonged to Patton's organization, others to higher or lower echelons. They were all engaged in the business of information. They brought in and carried out messages reporting on the situation, that is, telling what was happening at the time at various places along the front as it was known, noted, and interpreted at the different levels of command. The purpose was to keep everyone up to date on the fluid and ever-changing scene of the war.

In the hectic pace of the combat action and in the pressing search for immediacy, much was unknown and guessed at. Some knowledge thus disseminated was consequently inaccurate, out of context, or incomplete.

Wallace undoubtedly used at least some of this paperwork to refresh his memory when he was writing his book. Although he attained verisimilitude in his prose—all of it sounds right and above reproach—his view in large measure is necessarily fragmentary, and some of his facts are incorrect. He simply was unable in many cases to establish the reality of who had performed what on the battlefield.

What Wallace lacked and needed, above all, was access to the official records of the campaign. Unfortunately, they were unavailable to him.

Army Regulations, known as ARs, the code of laws governing the military establishment, provided for preserving the historical sources of the war so that valid histories could be written later. To this end, the ARs instructed all the major headquarters in the chain of command—that is to say, theater, army group, army, corps, division, regiment, and the more-or-less separate and independent battalions like artillery, engineer, quartermaster, medical, and others—to prepare a monthly After Action Report. This consisted of a narrative account of activities from the commander's point of view, together with supporting documents, namely journals, publications, and miscellaneous papers. Every month, each headquarters submitted these documents to the next higher command echelon, which, in turn, forwarded the papers up again. They ended in the custody of the Historian of the European Theater of Operations.

Starting in the summer of 1945, immediately after hostilities, and lasting about a year, military historians drawn from the field armies and gathered in Paris used these basic sources to write preliminary histories of the war in Europe. In the middle of 1946, shortly after Wallace's book appeared in print, these records, the bulk filling an entire railroad freight car, were on the way to the United States. Guarded by an escort officer and a crew of enlisted men, traveling aboard a Liberty ship, the collection reached the National Archives in Washington, D.C. There, the papers were sorted, categorized, labeled, and held for the U.S. Army's Chief of Military History.

These sources formed the basis of the official histories written in the Office of the Chief of Military History by military officers and civil servants. Eventually, the Government Printing Office published eighty-five books. Called the *U.S. Army in World War II*, the series details for the general public what occurred in every theater of operations during the war. It has been an incomparable reference for countless individuals who have studied the war ever since.

Wallace was unable to consult the official records, but, unfortunately, he was unaware of or overlooked another excellent source then in existence. This was an official Third Army history, published internally in Regensburg, Germany on May 13, 1945, a week after the war's end. Printed by the 652d Engineer Topographical Battalion and by Company B of 942d Engineer Topographical Battalion, which had facilities to render maps and texts, two massive tomes were entitled "Third Army Action Report." Prepared during the campaign by the Third Army's Historical Section, the first volume contains a daily narrative of the combat action; the second consists of supporting documents—letters of instruction, periodic operations and intelligence reports, graphs, and the like. The work is an impeccable record of events.

Without these documents, Wallace goes astray in several areas. He provides an operational framework or strategic outlook for the Allied activity. Nor does he furnish an overall plan for the German side of the struggle.

A more serious flaw is his lack of understanding of what was happening outside the confines of the Third Army. As a consequence, he fails to note the function of Gen. Omar N. Bradley who commanded the 12th Army Group headquarters immediately above Patton's Third Army. Bradley, after heading the First U.S. Army during the initial seven weeks of the invasion, turned over his command to Gen. Courtney Hodges and stepped up to take the army group on August 1, 1944. There he directed and coordinated, at first, Hodge's and Patton's armies, then also the Ninth and Fifteenth Armies commanded, respectively, by Gens. William Simpson and Leonard Gerow.

Wallace never mentions orders originating at army group and determining the Third Army's course of action. He makes Patton out to be an independent and autonomous figure. According to Wallace, Patton simply decided what he wanted to do, then went about and did it. In actuality, Patton, a stickler for military obedience and a disciplined soldier, always carried out the wishes of his superior, Bradley, who was at first under Gen. Sir Bernard L. Montgomery, the temporary Allied ground forces commander at 21st Army Group, later under Gen. Dwight D. Eisenhower, the Supreme Allied Commander. Those above Patton in the chain of command set his goals; Patton decided how to attain them.

Altogether false, Wallace terms as a Patton creation the Cobra attack from St. Lo to Avranches, the breakthrough that became breakout. It was actually Bradley's plan and execution. Bradley drew Patton into the offensive by asking him unofficially—the Third Army was still inactive and non-operational on the continent—to look after the VIII Corps late in July, for VIII Corps was scheduled to go under Patton when the Third Army headquarters opened for active campaigning on August 1. Bradley asked Hodges to do the same for the VII Corps slated to stay in the First Army when Hodges took control of it. Bradley's motive was to insure an easy and smooth transition into the new command structure effective at the beginning of August.

To Wallace, surrounding the Germans west of the Seine River by closing the Falaise pocket was Patton's idea, decision, and execution. Actually, Bradley had the notion, gained the approval of Eisenhower, who happened to be visiting him, and telephoned Montgomery to suggest the maneuver. Montgomery was in agreement and ordered Bradley to carry it out. Bradley instructed Patton to do so.

Smaller errors in Wallace's story abound. The invention of hedge cutters and the decision to weld them to the front of tanks to get them through the hedgerows in Normandy was not Patton's, but rather Bradley's. The use of heavy bombers in direct support of ground troops was not the first time, as Wallace says, the Allies had used the technique; they employed strategic bombers in this role earlier in Italy, at Monte Cassino and at Cassino, and then again at Caen. Not Nijmegen but rather Arnhem was the place where Allied troops tried vainly to cross the Rhine River in Holland in September 1944. The V Corps under First Army, not a Provisional Corps, as Wallace stated, liberated Paris

And finally, no mention is made of the attempt on Hitler's life on July 20. No explanation is given for the theater-wide supply crisis that halted the Allied advance toward the Siegfried Line in September 1944. No account is provided of Eisenhower's conference at Sedan to determine how to counter the Germans in the Battle of the Bulge.

There are numerous minor errors scattered across the pages of Wallace's book, but in the final analysis, the mistakes matter little and are relatively unimportant. They are more than balanced by Wallace's matchless capture of Third Army's glorious sweep across western Europe.

Tied in with that march to glory is what someone has called Wallace's "adulatory perspective of Patton." Wallace's feelings for and picture of Patton are neither peculiar nor out of place; they are true and real. Everyone associated with Patton came under his spell. Wallace dedicates his book to "our beloved commander," and he means the adjective literally. He goes on to say, "Anyone who ever worked closely with him would have died for him." This again is no offhand statement. The mystique of Patton bound him intimately to his troops who, throughout Patton's career, felt privileged to serve him. For, to quote Wallace again, Patton was "not only a great general but also a great man" whose presence "broadened our hopes and colored and enriched our lives."

A small group of friends, veterans of Patton's Third Army, sat in a cafe in Paris shortly before Christmas 1945, and talked about their ex-boss. They had just learned of his death in Germany, and it was difficult for some, impossible for the others to remain dry-eyed and hold back their tears.

Wallace's remarkable memoir initiated a series of books detailing Patton's character and military expertise, his will power and flamboyance. Harry Semmes, Patton's close friend and fellow warrior, a tanker in both world wars; Charles R. Codman, Patton's aide-de-camp in the Second World War; Robert S. Allen, Patton's former Deputy Assistant Chief of Staff, G-2 (Intelligence) in Europe; and Fred Ayers, Jr., Patton's nephew; in their books animated and fixed over the years Patton's generalship and personality.

By then, Patton was renowned, known to all. He became a legend, characterized as the "outstanding exponent of combat effectiveness in World War II." As for his Third Army, Eisenhower had blessed it with the highest praise. "You have made your Army," he told Patton, "a fighting force that is not excelled . . . by any other of equal size in the world."

Wallace had anticipated the kudos. He was sure of Patton's enduring place in history and, together with its chief, the Third Army. Both man and organization had performed with the highest efficiency, and both had gained and deserved the highest pinnacle of fame.

Martin Blumenson

Preface

THE powerful Third Army with its famous leader, General George S. Patton, Jr., which in ten months roared through France, Belgium, Luxembourg, Germany, Czechoslovakia and Austria, crushing at every turn the German war machine which in 1940-42 was considered the most powerful army in the world, have now passed into history. Before the memory of the great days of these campaigns as well as the close association with this famous American fighter grow dim, it might be interesting to jot down the story of the events as they unfolded and a few personal impressions of our leader.

This therefore is the story of The Third Army and its great commander.

General Patton had his neck broken in an automobile accident in Germany on 9 December 1945. Although almost completely paralyzed, he fought gamely, but finally succumbed on 20 December 1945—a year almost to the day after his Third Army's famous dash of over a hundred miles to the north to smash into the southern flank of Von Rundstedt's Ardennes offensive in Luxembourg and Belgium—the Battle of the Bulge.

Shortly before his death he stated: "This is a hell of a way to die."

Although millions mourned his going, no one, including himself, would have wanted him to have lived a cripple. As someone so aptly said, "he had finished his work." He, himself, felt and frequently said that "America cannot escape her destiny, and that destiny is to be great." He certainly had helped in no small way to make this country fulfill its destiny.

After his death eulogies were heaped upon him, not only from Americans, but from all over the world.

A typical editorial was that of 22 December 1945, in the Toronto, Canada, *Evening Telegram:*

"With the death of George S. Patton there passes from the scene one of the great soldiers of the last war and one of the most brilliant field commanders of all time. A leader of rare daring and impetuous energy, he showed around Metz and on the Moselle a tenacity that matched the audacity of his thrusts through France, Belgium and Germany. The success of his dazzling drives—as when he jumped the Rhine—was to be attributed as much to shrewd advance preparation as to the quickness of his eye for an opening. In the time to come his name will be a familiar one to all students of the military history that was made in the pre-atomic era.

"In that time the idiosyncracies which made him a subject of controversy and almost marred his career will appear of little importance in comparison with the soldierly qualities which made him one of the most successful and one of the most feared of the Allied generals.

"Canadians, who join with Americans in admiration of his leadership, will join with them in regret at his death."

After his untimely death, Mrs. Patton decided that his body should be buried along side the soldiers who had served under him, in the cemetery at Hamm, Luxembourg, along the storied route of the powerful Third Army drive to victory.

In the following pages I attempt to tell the story of this drive as seen from the Headquarters Third Army.

Having gone to the United Kingdom in July 1942, I witnessed the gradual build-up of our aerial might month after month and the increasing power of our blows from the air along with those of the Royal Air Force, of course, against Germany.

I also witnessed, and took part in the build-up of equipment and supplies and finally of our Ground Forces in the United Kingdom at the same time. There was one difference, however. As the air forces built up, the air blows increased simultaneously, while our ground forces continued to build up in strength and numbers, but no ground blows were struck until everything was ready. Then like lightning the ground forces were let loose at one time. From that time on Germany was given no respite.

As our great leader said before the Invasion:

"We shall attack and attack until we are exhausted, and then we shall attack again."

Philadelphia
September 1945-January 1946

1

The Two "Greatest Bluffs in History"

FOR many months through 1942 and 1943 the United States Army Air Forces, together with Britain's Royal Air Force, both operating from the British Isles, gained in strength and numbers. Slowly but surely they were knocking the German Luftwaffe out of the skies and dealing body blows to the cities and industries of Germany.

Each day we read in the papers of the increasing number of bombers and the damage they were inflicting in "round the clock" bombing of vital targets. The R.A.F. dropped thousands of tons of bombs by night and our own precision bombers dropped more thousands by day.

Eight hundred planes today, a thousand tomorrow, and still they came. The losses, we were told, were small, and so they were, proportionately. Only 46 planes last night, 52 today—only five or six per cent. But we couldn't avoid a quick figuring up; 52 planes gone, each with nine or ten highly-trained American or English crews, gone forever.

But we were told, too, that the destruction they wrought in Germany was terrific, and that "one of these days" Germany would realize she could stand no more and would capitulate. Magazine articles were written about it, commentators prophesied it and finally books appeared, all to prove that Germany could be defeated by air power alone.

However, the days rolled on into months and the

months into two years and still, although obviously badly hurt by the air blows, Germany showed no real sign of quitting. We were forced to fight bitterly for Africa and Sicily and the Allied armies found the going slow in Italy.

As time passed and the pounding of Germany from the air continued, the rumor spread that no ground invasion of the Continent would ever be made because it would not be necessary. Air power would do it all. Many believed this at the time. The tremendous flow of men and materiel from the United States to the British Isles for many long and tedious months was called "the greatest bluff in history."

But it wasn't a bluff. June 6, 1944, dawned and the world was electrified by the news that the American First Army and British and Canadian forces had successfully attacked the beaches of Normandy, had landed and had penetrated inland against almost insurmountable obstacles—mines, steel barriers, gun emplacements and every other device that a determined and crafty enemy had been able to construct during the two-year wait.

It was touch-and-go for several days, but finally a substantial sector of the coast was held securely and the Allied world breathed a little easier.

The Germans were breathing uneasily. Anxiously their High Command checked the reports from spies in England and from Intelligence Units in Normandy to discover what reserves the Allies had. They knew that one corps of General George S. Patton, Jr's, Third Army, the VIII, had been attached to the First Army for the invasion, but that most of his Third Army still were in England. It was in connection with them that the second of the "greatest bluffs in history" occurred.

We knew that General Eisenhower, the Supreme Allied Commander, had the highest esteem for General Patton and his Third Army, and we had heard that the Germans,

2

having felt his quality in Sicily, feared him greatly. But we did not then know why Third Army Headquarters was left near the little town of Knutsford, a few miles south of Manchester and why our troops were scattered through England and North Ireland for more than three weeks after the invasion started.

It was part of the "cover plan," as it was called. Keeping General Patton and his army where they were, and being sure to let the German agents find out that they were there, constituted such a threat to Germany, and her leaders so feared a direct thrust by the Third Army at some other point, that they kept 17 divisions along the Pas de Calais section of the Channel coast, afraid to use them as reinforcements in Normandy.

So realistically was this "cover plan" carried out that each day ships on the east coast were loaded with troops and just at dusk they moved out into the Channel while it was still light enough for German observation planes to see them. Then, after darkness settled, they moved back again into port and unloaded.

Thus a double purpose was served. Troops and the crews of the ships had valuable training in quick loading and unloading, and a new battle had been won in the war of nerves we were waging against the Germans. They never could be sure whether a new invasion was really under way or whether it was just another bluff. In some cases where reinforcements actually were being sent the First Army in Normandy the ships would move into the Channel just before dark as if heading for a new point of invasion, then under cover of darkness would change course to head for the Normandy beaches. By such deceptive measures, the Germans were fooled completely.

On 28 June, the Third Army finally got orders to move. Secretly we slipped quietly and quickly down into southern England.

Third Army Headquarters was set up in Braemer House and several other old manor houses just south of Salisbury. When we left, and for several weeks after we had arrived in France, radios and signal equipment belonging to our headquarters remained in place at Knutsford and were kept in operation exactly as if the full headquarters still was operating there. In fact, some of the signal equipment was moved closer to the eastern coast of England to throw the Germans further off the trail.

The long, cool, clear English summer evenings were ideal for relaxing, but nothing was further from our minds. The very air was tense. We were trained and ready. We knew that the shifting of headquarters presaged action. We tried to relax and keep calm. It was not easy.

Late in the afternoon of 3 July, we got word that there would be a staff meeting of Section Chiefs of the Headquarters at 1730 hours.* It was an unusual time for a staff meeting.

We assembled quietly. There was little of the usual talk as we waited for General Patton.

Exactly at the appointed time of 1730, General Patton strode quickly but quietly in and took his place before us. For just a moment his glance roved over the ranks of his staff, the men who would be carrying out and putting into effect his battle orders. Then he spoke:

"Gentlemen, the moment for which we have all been working and training so long has at last arrived. Tomorrow we go to war! I congratulate you. And I prophesy that your names and the name of the Third Army will go down in history—or they will go down in the records of the Graves Registration Bureau. Thank you. Good-night!"

The Third Army was "on the roll"!

---

*5:30 P. M. The Army and Navy use the Continental 24-hour time system.

2

The Preparation and Build Up

CHURCHILL called Great Britain an "Unsinkable Aircraft Carrier." So it proved to be during the Battle of Britain, but it proved to be even more of an "Unsinkable Troop Carrier" during 1942, 1943 and early 1944. It was the base at which the Allied forces were built up for the invasion of the continent, and from which the assault on fortress Europe was launched in June 1944 in conjunction with the Russian drive from the east, to topple the Nazi Empire.

Early in 1942, several thousand American combat troops went to North Ireland, prepared to help ward off any German invasion. In addition to these combat troops, ETOUSA (European Theater of Operations United States Army) Headquarters was set up in London to work with the British in planning the invasion, and the reception and supply of all American troops to be used in that theater. At a later date SHAEF (Supreme Headquarters Allied Expeditionary Forces) Headquarters was set up which was the overall planning and combat command of the Allied invasion forces. General Dwight D. Eisenhower was the Commander of ETOUSA and later also of SHAEF. In the latter headquarters there were approximately half British and half American officers. The section heads alternated, American and British, and under each one was a deputy of the opposite nationality.

General Eisenhower was an ideal choice for Supreme

Commander. The great British field marshal, later Viceroy of India, Sir Archibald Wavell, once said: "The statesman or politician, who has to persuade and confute, must keep an open and flexible mind, accustomed to criticism and argument; the mind of the soldier, who commands and obeys without question is apt to be fixed, drilled, and attached to definite rules—That each should understand the other better is essential for the conduct of modern war." General Eisenhower proved to be a diplomat and a statesman, as well as a soldier.

Under General Eisenhower, two plans were devised, both with code names. The first was called BOLERO—the concentration of troops, equipment and supplies in the United Kingdom (UK). The other was called OVERLORD—the plan for the invasion.

The actual crossing of the Channel, after the ships had been loaded, was called NEPTUNE. This was under the command of the British Admiralty. The other two were combined British and American army operations. All were, of course, under the Supreme Commander, General Eisenhower.

The combined forces in Great Britain for the invasion were approximately 650,000 U. S. combat forces; 425,000 U. S. service forces; and approximately 650,000 British and Canadian combat forces in addition to their service troops.

There were also some French, Polish and other Allied forces from various countries.

For purposes of administration, the UK was divided into several Base Sections or Commands and our Service Forces followed in general the British administrative organization. There was an Eastern Base, a Southern Base, and a Western Base Section. There was also a North Ireland Base Section, comprising the six counties of North Ireland; and then there was the Central Base Section, which took in only London and its suburbs.

Many installations in these Base Sections, such as warehouses, camps, ordnance shops, hospitals, etc., were turned over completely to the Americans. Others were built by us. But many of the ports, such as Liverpool and Glasgow, were operated jointly. Some of the ports along the very southern coast of England, from which the invasion was to be launched, were kept strictly under the Admiralty. In fact some of the coast along the south, and some along the east and far in the north in Scotland, was forbidden territory, so secret were the activities going on there. Two of these secrets have been revealed as Operation MULBERRY, the famous floating docks that made it possible to supply the invasion forces, and Operation PLUTO, Pipeline Under The Ocean, which kept the Third Army supplied with fuel in their dash across Europe.

Large covered tanks were constructed on the Isle of Wight, just off the southern coast of England, in which enormous quantities of gasoline could be stored. They were connected by 5-inch pipes to the southern ports of England, where tankers docked and pumped the gasoline directly through the pipes to them.

From the Isle of Wight other pipes of the same size were laid on the floor of the Channel, extending across until they were close to the coast of France. After the invasion was successful and the port of Cherbourg was captured, the pipes were continued right up onto the land. Composition pipes, bolted together in sections, were then run along the surface of the ground and followed General Patton's motorized columns as they dashed all over France. It was only the constant supply of tank and truck fuel brought by this means right up behind our lines that enabled us to travel so fast and so far.

In the build-up in England, one of the biggest problems was the housing of the million-odd American troops. In solving this problem we also worked closely with the British. They furnished the bulk of the accommodations, although some of the buildings were prefabricated ones brought from America and erected by our own Engineers. Our Engineers also built many complete air fields and roads. Most of the camps, hospitals, warehouses, etc., were either converted buildings which had been remodeled by the British or brand new camps erected by their Engineers. By the time all the American troops for the invasion had arrived, in addition to the Canadians and the British forces, every available building, new and old, was filled to capacity, many tent camps were in operation and thousands of troops were billeted on the populace.

Great Britain and Ireland are most attractive and beautiful, as anyone who has been there knows. The peoples were delightfully pleasant and cordial to us and welcomed us like long lost relatives. They were hospitable and cooperative, and endeavored in every possible way to make us feel at home in their country. Our relations with the British army were also cordial and cooperative. It was no easy matter for two armies to be quartered and trained in a small, congested country such as England without friction, but as far as I know, there was scarcely an unpleasant incident between the two in all the months that our troops were there. They used to call us "the great American Army of Occupation," but that was only in fun. A large part of the credit for this congenial and warm feeling between our soldiers and the soldiers and civilians of Great Britain was due to the feelings shown at the top, between our Governments and high Army officers, and particularly the orders and indoctrination issued by our Supreme Theater Commander.

Every American soldier, within 48 hours of his arrival at his station in the UK was given what was called an indoctrination lecture on four subjects—1. Security;

2. Passes, Leaves and Furloughs; 3. Relations with the British; and 4. The Color Question.

No man could leave camp until he had been indoctrinated on these subjects.

Security was, of course, most important as we were then only a few miles across the Channel from the enemy. However, the two subjects most drilled into the officers and men were, that there were to be cordial relations established with the British, and that there was to be no color line drawn between our colored and white troops.

Each officer and enlisted man was impressed with the fact that he was a personal representative of the United States Army in his relations and dealings with the British people, civilian as well as military. All troops were instructed that, instead of their arriving in a "foreign country," they were themselves, in the eyes of the British people, the "foreigners" arriving in the British homeland and living among the people of that land, and that their conduct must be of the same high standard that they would require were the situation reversed.

It was pointed out that the United Kingdom had been a nation at war for more than four years and conditions there were vastly different from those of peace. There were relatively few households that had not sustained family or financial losses. The pay scale of the American soldier was higher than that of the British, our rations more elaborate and more recreational facilities had been provided. It was ordered that comparisons would not be made or discussed.

England has a somewhat cold, damp climate, but it has compensations, we found, for the summers were delightfully cool. There were practically no flies, mosquitoes or other insects and the climate was quite healthful. In summer, daylight lasted until almost midnight and it got

9

light again at 3 or 4 o'clock in the morning, due of course to the northern latitude and double daylight saving.

They say a foreign country is a place where everything is funny but the jokes. A story was told of an American soldier who met a pretty English girl and said to her: "Hello, Sweetheart, where have you been all my life?" And she proceeded to tell him.

We soon found, however, that the English had a keen and subtle humor and a pleasing conversation. Many of the words they used were different from ours, but we soon understood each other.

All in all, the old saying "England and America are two similar countries, separated by a common language," did not seem to work out.

One of the most novel aids to speed the build-up was the decision of our High Command for all of our combat units to leave in the U. S. practically all the quartermaster and ordnance equipment they had been using during their training in the United States. The men alone, with their personal gear and some light, scarce articles of equipment, were loaded on the ships for overseas.* This accomplished several things. It enabled heavy, and in fact all kinds of equipment, guns, tanks, trucks, etc., to be shipped and stored in England months in advance while our troops were still training and consuming rations at home.

When they arrived overseas the units were issued fine new equipment of every description, all of the latest design, ready for the rigors of what proved to be a long and strenuous campaign.

In addition to our build-up of combat and service troops in England, our Replacement (later called Reinforcement) System was organized and started to function. The system used was quite different from that used in

---

*This did not apply to those troops which went directly to Africa in November 1942. These were "combat loaded" on this side because they entered immediately into combat when they landed.

World War I, where units which had suffered heavy casualties were taken out of the line for rest and reorganization, and other whole units sent in to relieve them.

In this war, large Replacement Training Centers were established and after hostilities had commenced, a large Replacement Depot was located in each Army area, fairly well to the rear. Each Depot had attached to it several Replacement Battalions. Troops of all classifications, infantrymen, artillerymen, tankmen, radio operators, technicians of all descriptions, were fed from the Training Centers into the Depots and from there into the Replacement Battalions. In this way, when a front line unit needed replacements, due to casualties of one kind or another, it put a requisition direct to its Corps Replacement Battalion for the needed number of men of certain specified categories. Unless the Corps Battalion was low in "stock", as it was called, the replacements would arrive in a matter of a few hours. In this way, it was possible to keep units at full strength, or nearly so, at all times. It also explains why it was possible for some divisions to remain in continuous combat for 9 and 10 months at a time.

In order that those men who were not casualties could get a much needed rest at times, a few individuals, or small groups and sometimes small or medium units would frequently be taken out of the line, particularly if the situation warranted it, and sent back to the rear areas for a few days rest and recreation. It was in taking care of these combat troops, back a few miles from the front for a short rest, that our Red Cross did some of its best work. There were frequently no other healthful places for rest and recreation for these boys, except the Red Cross Centers set up in the towns behind the lines. Here they could write home, play games, get some hot coffee and food and talk to their buddies and the Red Cross workers before returning to their places in the battle line.

The date for the big invasion had been tentatively set for May or June 1944. Several weeks before the earliest possible date, Operation OVERLORD—the plan for the invasion—went into effect. This plan had been worked out by a Joint Planning Committee of British and American officers.

Everything about OVERLORD had to be done with the greatest secrecy. Those in the know, who had the top secret information, were comparatively few, and were sworn to silence. Only a handful of the highest officers in England had all, or nearly all, of the real information. No one, not even Eisenhower, had the date of D Day, for he himself did not set it until almost the time.

For weeks beforehand, stores and supplies were accumulated in the vicinity of the debarkation ports by the Base Sections SOS (Service of Supply), for the Americans, and the equivalent British commands for the British. The British Movement Control and the U. S. Transportation Corps handled all of the troop movements and schedules, either by train or road in the UK. Liaison was constant at this time between the military and the civil authorities—police, fire, etc.—and with the navy.

The defense of this great movement chiefly A.A., smoke and fire-fighting units—rested with the British. The British also took care of all signal communications during this period.

All organizational equipment was marked with the unit serial number, the unit color stripes and the cubic feet and weight. Movement tables and troop lists were prepared.

The troops were divided into the Assault and the Build-Up forces. The Assault were the troops which made the actual assault landing across the beaches of Normandy. After these followed the Build-Up troops, which reinforced and maintained the Allied Expeditionary Forces.

All troops initially passed through the Concentration

Area. For some this might be their original home camp, for others a camp closer to the southern ports of England. From this Concentration Area, units moved by either rail or road to the Marshalling Areas. Units might remain here up to 2 weeks, usually 4 to 6 days. In these Marshalling Areas Static Forces cooked meals for the troops. This was called "hotel services." The final markings were completed, defective vehicles replaced, all vehicles were waterproofed so that they could land in salt water and not be ruined, and troops were broken down into unit parties and formed into craft loads.

From the Marshalling Areas, units then moved into the Embarkation Areas. This move was made under their own power over the roads, by craft or ship loads. In these Embarkation Areas were usually located a number of Embarkation Points—docks or improvised concrete docks for landing craft—called "Hards." In the Embarkation Area, final preparations were completed. Time there varied from a couple of hours to 2 days. There the troops were briefed, the Landing Ration (a type of K ration sufficient for 24 hours) and an Emergency Ration (chocolate reinforced with vitamins) were issued. A final hot meal was fed and the troops were ready to go aboard ship.

The time on shipboard was estimated as 48 hours, sometimes it was less. On shipboard Sea Passage Rations and vomit bags were issued.

The actual mileage from the ports of southern England to the beaches of Normandy was about 100 miles.

3

The Staff—Headquarters Third U. S. Army

BEFORE giving some facts about the Staff of Head-quarters Third U. S. Army, it might be well to explain briefly what an Army is, and of what it is composed. The basic large combat unit is a division. There are three main types of divisions—Infantry, approximate strength 14,200; Armored, 10,723; and Airborne, 8,500. There are also special divisions organized for specific purposes—Mountain Divisions, Ski Divisions, etc.

The next higher organization is a Corps. A Corps consists of a Corps Headquarters to which are attached 2 or more divisions of any type, plus additional troops, such as artillery, engineers, quartermaster, medical, tank destroyer, cavalry, ordnance, etc.

The Army is the next higher organization and consists of an Army Headquarters and 2 or more Corps, plus a large number of separate groups and battalions of the same varying types as in a Corps. These separate units usually equal approximately the same number as the total number of troops in the divisions. In other words, if the number of troops in the divisions of the Army at any one time totaled say, 165,000, then the Corps and Army troops would probably total about 165,000 or a grand total in the whole Army of 330,000 troops. Some of these separate units remain as Army troops, directly under the control of Army Headquarters, while others are attached from time to time to the various Corps. There is nothing permanent about either an Army or a Corps, except its Headquarters organization. Units are frequently switched back and forth between Corps and also between Armies. Some units, however, may remain with the same parent headquarters throughout a campaign or even throughout a whole war, as several of ours did from the time they were assigned to us in England until the last shot was fired in Austria and Czechoslovakia.

In addition to the ground forces assigned to an Army, a Tactical Air Force is also assigned for air support and reconnaissance. Squadrons of this Tactical Air Force are daily assigned to duty with each Corps of the Army.

The next higher organization above the Army is the Army Group. This is composed of 2 or more Armies.

Above the Army Group is the Supreme Headquarters of the Theater of Operations.

All headquarters have approximately the same organization. At the top, of course, is the Commanding General, who alone is responsible for all that his organization does or fails to do. Directly under him is the Chief of Staff, who is the Commander's chief assistant and the coordinator of the staff. He in turn has a Deputy as his assistant.

The Staff itself is divided into four principal sections. These are called General Staff Sections—G-1; G-2; G-3; and G-4. G-1 is responsible for Personnel; G-2 for Military Intelligence; G-3 for Operations and Training; and G-4 for Supply and Evacuation. In large headquarters there has recently also been added a G-5 who has charge of Civil Affairs, Displaced Persons, etc.

In addition to the General Staff group there is also a Special Staff group consisting of all other staff sections, including specialists and heads of services. Included in this group are: Air Officer, Adjutant General, Antiaircraft, Artillery, Chaplain, Chemical, Engineer, Finance,

Headquarters Commandant, Inspector General, Judge Advocate, Liaison, Ordnance, Provost Marshal, Quartermaster, Signal, and Surgeon.

The Staff assists the Commander in the exercise of command. It collects information, makes plans, arranges details and makes recommendations. A well organized staff must coordinate activities; its members must work in harmony and consult and inform each other.

The qualifications of a good staff officer are—ability, tact, the confidence of the Commander, courageous frankness and loyalty.

The Tables of Organization call for 244 officers and 800 enlisted men in an Army Staff. Actually, when the Third Army got into operation across France it had a total of 801 officers alone. This included all of the attached officers, of course—air, O.S.S., military government detachments, French, English, etc. who were a part of, and traveled with our headquarters. Counting all of the necessary units which were a part of our headquarters such as Signal Battalion, Tank Destroyer Battalion, AAA Battalion, Cavalry Squadron, Ordnance Co., Military Police, etc., the whole headquarters totaled between 3,500 and 4,500.

When it is realized that for the first 5 or 6 weeks of our dash across France from Normandy almost to the German border we traveled over 500 miles, moving every 3 or 4 days with jumps of 20 to 80 miles each time, it can be seen that the Headquarters had to be fairly mobile.

During my army career I have been a member of many staffs, among them three Army (one British), a Corps, two Base, and two Divisions, but in all my experience I have never worked on a Staff that could compare to that of Third U. S. Army. Some headquarters are like merry-go-rounds. You feel as though you are going in circles, so many motions are superfluous. This was particularly true in the Base headquarters where so much was done for appearance and for effect. Everyone tried to appear busy but actually a lot of the activity was wasteful and inefficient. The appearance of activity was frequently designed to impress someone higher up and the job was really a clock-punching one.

Not so in Third Army Headquarters, however. Nothing was done there for show or appearance. Everything was practical and for a purpose. The "Old Man" hated show and sham. He was interested in one thing only—efficiency; and his spirit permeated the whole organization. You had a feeling that Third Army was going in only one direction—forward.

All members of the Staff would willingly work all hours of the day or night if necessary to get a job done. But if our individual work was caught up, we could relax and josh each other and enjoy ourselves, without the slightest fear that anyone would criticise us for not being busy. A number of persons have asked if General Patton was not very difficult to work for, always driving you on. He was just the opposite and as I mentioned, his spirit carried through the whole staff. Everything around Headquarters was quiet, orderly, smooth and efficient.

Whether in tents in the field, or in buildings, it was like working in a large and very efficient business organization. The Old Man would not tolerate unnecessary noise or confusion. You either knew your job, or you didn't. If you didn't, or if you were the cause of any friction in the Headquarters, you were quickly and quietly gotten rid of, "rolled" as we called it—sent to some other organization. But if you knew your job you were allowed to perform it in your own way and were never told how to do a thing, only requested in a quiet gentlemanly way to do it. The rest was up to you. Results were all that counted.

There were few rules about the Headquarters but these

were, of course, expected to be obeyed. When outside of quarters we were ordered to wear steel helmets, side arms, and field uniform. We were at breakfast before 0730 and at our offices either in tents or buildings, every morning by o800. This applied to Sundays as well as all holidays while we were in combat. There were no exceptions. Normally we were free to go to our quarters after dinner in the evening, although as I have said, many times we worked well into the night. We were considered on duty 24 hours of every day. If we were absent, someone had to be on hand in our Section, in case of emergency. Our whereabouts was also known so that we could be reached if necessary. This of course was only good staff procedure.

No unnecessary words were uttered, only a word or two of praise from time to time for a job particularly well done.

Most of the Staff, particularly the Chiefs of Sections, were a group of individualists. No two were alike, but all fine officers and most interesting and pleasant to work with. Each knew his own job and worked perfectly in harmony with the other.

My own assignment in the Headquarters was Assistant Chief of Staff G-3 Liaison. I was responsible for locating and placing in covered accommodations all Third Army troops, numbering some 325,000 throughout the United Kingdom. Again in Normandy, in the unbelievably congested area of the Cherbourg Peninsula, all Third Army units had to be placed in fields, orchards and woods, physically suitable and at the same time in conformity with the tactical plan, permitting the uninterrupted flow of all types of troops not only from the beaches but also through the historic breakthrough at Avranches. Beginning in early October when the Third Army halted at the Moselle, it once more became necessary to locate covered accommodations for 400,000 troops (some 500 separate units). In addition, many other units and personnel had to be accommodated in the Third Army area. This included Air Force, Communications Zone, French, British, Belgian and Luxembourg units, prisoners of war, and countless civilian refugees and displaced persons. The closest staff coordination was necessary as well as the fullest cooperation with French, Belgian and Luxembourg civil and military authorities. Because of the scarcity of suitable housing in war-torn areas, and at times the severe winter, meticulous planning was necessary, especially in securing adequate hospitalization for battle casualties.

My most interesting and exciting work, however, was probably the organization and operation of the Liaison Section.

Liaison—the connecting link between units—is vital in combat. Properly conducted, it is the human link by which distant headquarters are kept constantly informed of important developments as they occur. The Liaison Section is the information center of a headquarters. It must work closely with G-2 and G-3 and the Chief of Staff to insure that the commanding general is provided with the most complete, accurate, and up-to-date information available. However, the Liaison Section must secure information of essential interest to all staff sections, as G-4, Supply, for instance. This information must all be passed on to the interested section without delay.

In this Liaison Section, besides officers in Third Army Headquarters, were officers attached to Twelfth Army Group and adjacent Armies, First Army on the north and Seventh on the south. Twelfth Army Group and each adjacent Army in turn assigned Liaison officers to Third Army Headquarters. In addition, each Corps also sent two or more officers. Furthermore, on numerous occasions, separate divisions were ordered to establish liaison with Army, and frequently French, British, and Belgian officers were also present. All of these officers operated under the Chief Liaison Officer and their reports had to be screened and the information disseminated.

Information to be of value must be accurate and it must arrive swiftly. A commanding general based his decisions not alone on what he, himself, has seen, but on the information gathered for him, from various fronts, by his liaison officers.

General Patton demanded that the most up-to-date information be at his Headquarters from all units on all fronts at 0800 and again at 1600. The General was briefed at 0900 and again at 1700. At the 0900 briefing, all the Chiefs of Sections were present and our front line situation —as reported by information received from liaison officers, Corps G-2 and G-3 reports or possibly a late phone call from a Corps or a short wave radio pick-up—was explained by G-3. The Air Officer next gave a short summary of events relative to the air arm. Then G-2 gave a briefing on the enemy intelligence situation, secured from the same sources as G-3. Finally a brief summary of the newscasts was also given as picked up from B.B.C., American stations, and short wave interceptions. All of the reports covered not only information on our own front, but also from the Armies on our flanks, the British, Canadians, French and Ninth U. S. Army as well as higher headquarters. There was news of course from Russia, the Pacific and in fact the whole world, but it was all brief and very much to the point.

The whole briefing, given in the War Room or Tent, where were kept up-to-date maps of the whole world, never lasted over 20 minutes. Immediately after this War Room briefing, the same information was given, taken from notes, to the 25 odd liaison officers collected in the liaison room or tent in front of the liaison situation maps. All the liaison officers took notes at this briefing and immediately thereafter went to their own headquarters to deliver the complete information there. So that by ap-

proximately noon each day, every unit of Third Army
had a summary of the complete situation and news from
every other front.

Following is a list of the officers of Third U. S. Army
Headquarters during the summer of 1944 and the spring
of 1945, giving the Chiefs of Section and in some cases
the executive officers:
Commanding General—General George S. Patton, Jr.
  Aide—Lt. Col. Charles R. Codman
  Aide—Major Alexander C. Stiller
  Personal Physician—Col. Charles B. Odom
Chief of Staff—Major General Hobart R. Gay
  (28 Jan.-1 April, 1944 and 10 Oct. 1944—Sept. 1945)
  Aide—Major George F. Murnane, Jr.
Chief of Staff—Maj. Gen. Hugh J. Gaffey
  (1 April, 1944-10 Oct., 1944)
  Aide—Capt. Elliott R. Taylor
  Aide—1st Lt. Allison C. Wysong, Jr.
Deputy Chief of Staff—Col. Paul D. Harkins
Sec. to General Staff—Lt. Col. George R. Pfann
Asst. Chief of Staff—G-1—Col. Frederick S. Mathews
  Executive—Lt. Col. William A. Horne, Jr.
Asst. Chief of Staff—G-2—Col. Oscar W. Koch
  Executive—Col. Robert S. Allen
Asst. Chief of Staff—G-3—Brig. Gen. Halley G. Maddox
  Executive—Col. William A. Borders
Asst. Chief of Staff—G-3 (Liaison)—Col. Brenton G.
  Wallace
  Executive—Lt. Col. John F. Wolf
Asst. Chief of Staff—G-4—Brig. Gen. Walter J. Muller
  Executive—Col. William H. Harrison
Asst. Chief of Staff—G-4 (Transportation)—Col. Redding
  F. Perry
Asst. Chief of Staff—G-5—Col. Nicholas W. Campanole
  Executive—Col. Roy L. Dafferes

21

Adjutant General—Col. Robert E. Cummings
Anti-Aircraft—Col. Frederick R. Chamberlain
Artillery—Brig. Gen. Edward T. Williams
Chaplain—Col. James H. O'Neill
Chemical—Col. Edward C. Wallington
Engineer—Brig. Gen. John F. Conklin
    Executive—Col. David H. Tulley
Finance—Col. Charles B. Milliken
Inspector General—Col. Clarence C. Park
Judge Advocate—Col. Charles E. Cheever
Medical—Brig. Gen. Thomas D. Hurley
    Executive—Col. John B. Coates, Jr.
Ordnance—Col. Thomas H. Nixon
    Executive—Col. David L. Van Syckle
Provost Marshal—Col. Philip C. Clayton
    Executive—Col. Harold Engerud
Quartermaster—Col. Everett Busch
    Executive—Col. Fenton M. Wood
Signal—Col. Elton F. Hammond
    Executive—Col. Claude E. Haswell
Special Service—Col. Kenneth E. Van Buskirk
Headquarters Commandant—Col. Rufus S. Bratton
    Executive—Col. Fred H. Kelley

4

Across the Beaches

AS mentioned at the end of Chapter I, Third Army
Headquarters received orders on 3 July 1944 that
on the following day, 4 July, it would secretly move
down from southern England, at Braemer House near
Salisbury, to the ports along the southern coast and em
bark for the beaches of Normandy.

By this date the American First Army and the British
and Canadians had captured the coast of Normandy from
the Orne River at Caen west. The beachheads established
by the British had, of course, been linked up with the
two American beachheads, "Utah" and "Omaha", on
either side of the Vire River, and the Americans had
driven across to the west coast of the Cotentin Peninsula
at Barneville and Carteret. Then the American VII Corps
(9th and 79th Divisions) had turned north to clean up
the whole of the peninsula and capture the most important
port of Cherbourg.

At this time therefore, the British and Canadians were
holding the eastern sector of the front from the coast
north of Caen, and the First U. S. Army with the V, XIX,
VII Corps, in that order from east to west, and the VIII
Corps, which had been attached from Third Army, were
holding the western sector of the front all the way to
the west coast near Lessay.

General Patton and his Chief of Staff were flown across
the Channel to France on 4 July. Late in the afternoon

of that same day, the Headquarters started by motor down to the port of Southhampton in the embarkation area, to board the ships for the passage across the Channel. As we neared the port, our column moved slower and slower, and finally came to a halt in the center of the city. Despite the light, we finally realized that it was almost midnight, and decided that we would probably be stuck there for the rest of the night. So we tried to make the best of it. We all had our own motor equipment, of course, for we had been made independently mobile for the campaign. I personally had my own jeep and trailer and my sergeant driver. All of my equipment, including my CP (Command Post) tent, bedding roll and other personal belongings, as well as those belonging to my driver, were in the trailer, covered with a tarpaulin.

Earlier in the evening we had become pretty hungry so opened some K rations and ate them for the first time. They were supposed to be full of vitamins, but to us they tasted terrible. Later on in France, we changed our minds and thought they were excellent. Some time after midnight, we located an army kitchen and got some hot coffee.

Some of us tried to sleep on the benches in a park, opposite which we were stopped, but I never realized how hard park benches really were. It got pretty cool toward morning and I finally crawled in under the tarpaulin on top of the baggage, in the trailer and got a little sleep

The following morning we drove our vehicles aboard an LST (Landing Ship Tank), which is larger than an LCT (Landing Craft Tank). Both have fronts which drop down as the vessel hits the beach, and the vehicles aboard run off the ship to the beach over the ramp. The LST has two decks, the upper one reached by a large elevator which carries vehicles from deck to deck.

The LST was equipped with triple-tier bunks and blankets for the enlisted men and junior officers. The senior officers had bunks in staterooms. The meals going across the Channel were hot, and were really excellent. The whole trip over was surprisingly comfortable.

It took practically all day for our ships to be loaded and our convoy formed and we did not sail till the night of 5 July. When we came on deck the next morning, it was a beautiful clear day and the Channel was quite a sight. In front of us and behind us, as far as the eye could see, were LST's, Liberty and Victory ships in double column plowing across the Channel. Each ship carried a silver barrage balloon, extending on a cable from its stern. It was really a bridge of ships. On either side of the double column, destroyers flitted here and there and off in the distance could occasionally be seen the low outline of a cruiser or a battleship.

As we neared the French coast we began to hear the rumble of guns, demolition charges along the coast, with once in awhile the explosion of a mine. As we approached Utah Beach we saw a great deal of wreckage, smashed craft and vehicles, and many underwater obstacles, although many of these things had been removed.

Our LST beached shortly after noon of 6 July and we drove ashore over the ramp formed by our dropped bow. The beach traffic was fairly well organized although dozens of ships were lined up on both sides of us discharging their loads onto the sand. We drove over a sort of highway marked by the vehicles along the beach and then up a ramp built through an opening in the sea wall onto the land above. Beach strong-points and enemy gun emplacements which had been captured or smashed, were of course visible everywhere. We began to see mine fields placed by the Heinies, marked with a scull and crossbones and the words "Achtung-Minen." They told us the white signs marked dummy mine fields and the yellow ones the real thing.

As we went inland we saw the barbed wire entanglements and the French gray stone houses which had been wrecked by the naval and artillery shells and also small fields of crosses where the dead had been buried. When we came to Ste. Mere Eglise and other towns we found that many civilians still lived there and they welcomed us warmly with smiles and hand waving and an occasional "Vive l'Amerique!" As we got farther inland they even offered us Calvados to drink and threw apples to us. One of the most amusing things, however, was to see the little children, six or seven years old, try to give us Churchill's famous victory sign made with the first two fingers of the hand. These little youngsters, having been taught the Nazi salute by the Heinies, and of course knowing no better, would first give us a stiff Nazi salute and then immediately open the two fingers making the "V" sign at the same time.

Those of us who had been in the First World War immediately remembered the war-torn France and the battle-front of those bygone days, as the same sights and sounds and smells greeted our senses. It seemed almost like a dream.

Our column moved rapidly inland to an assembly field where our vehicles were de-waterproofed, and then we moved to our headquarters area near the little town of Nehou, not far from St. Sauveur. Here we were all dispersed and camouflaged in fields and orchards, under canvas. We were near the center of the Cotentin Peninsula about 8 miles behind the front lines, almost in rear of VIII Corps, which was then attached to First Army. General Patton and his chief of staff lived in trailers or "caravans" as they were called, the other officers in wall or CP (Command Post) tents and the men in pup tents. We had large wall tents for each Section Headquarters. These were, of course, always well concealed under trees and camouflage nets.

During these first weeks of July, other Third Army troops were pouring across the Channel and funneling through Utah Beach, as we had done, onto the Cotentin

Peninsula, so overflowing that narrow neck of land that it was difficult to keep from being pushed into the front lines along with the First Army units that were slugging it out with the Heinies. Any intermingling with front line units had been expressly forbidden without authority of the Chief of Staff, for Patton and the Third Army, as far as the Germans (and even the troops of the First Army) were concerned, were still in Northern England. Any First or Third Army man captured might have let the cat out of the bag.

We were, however, as opportunity permitted, allowed to visit other places on the Peninsula and to learn all we could. We visited many of the so called "liberated" French towns, which had been so destroyed by our naval and artillery shells that scarcely a wall was left standing intact and not a single inhabitant remained in them. These were the towns which had been German strongholds and which had been stubbornly defended by them. Other towns were little or only partially destroyed. These were fully inhabited, in fact they were frequently overcrowded, as people from the destroyed towns moved into them. As the battle flowed through these towns the people frequently continued to live in the cellars, till it passed through, and then moved upstairs again.

It was most interesting to see our airfields built close behind the lines, frequently under shell and sometimes under small arms fire. Our bulldozers pulled out whole orchards and leveled the ground in a few hours. The surface of the runways was made firm and dry by scooping out a trench all the way along the edges, then placing a special heavy, tough tar paper over the surface and tucking it into the trenches along the edges. The tar paper was kept in place and taut by placing wire mesh on top of it, fastened securely with pegs.

Many of the bridges near the front were in range of enemy artillery and were frequently being shelled. Signs

27

would read "Bridge under fire! Keep 60 yard intervals. Keep moving!"

On the Cotentin Peninsula were dozens and dozens of rocket launching sites. Many of these had camouflaged concrete runways built like lanes or roads running to block houses which had been remodeled from old houses or barns. One of the most interesting was a very large one built for the launching of V-2's. It had enormous underground steel and concrete compartments and storage places, and the runways themselves were 1,000 feet long and were built in two slabs of reinforced concrete each 20 feet thick or a total of 40 feet of reinforced concrete.

Cherbourg, only recently fallen to the VII Corps of First Army, was a grim panorama of destruction, wrought not only by our own air forces and artillery before we captured the port, but also by German demolitions. By working around the clock at top speed our Base Section Engineers had the port fairly well cleared by the middle of July. One most upsetting thing, however, were the German time mines on the bottom of the harbor, which rose to just under the surface of the water at irregular periods. These clock devices, it was finally found, could be set for any period up to 3 weeks. The minesweepers would have the harbor all cleared one day, only to find the next day a number of new mines floating in the water.

Liberty and Victory ships, however, were lying at anchor in the outer harbor, being unloaded by "ducks," one of the developments that materially aided amphibious warfare. They were really 2½ ton trucks with the bodies constructed like boats. They operated either as trucks on land or as boats in the water.

The Liberty ships were unloaded rapidly by an ingenious method. Large cargo nets of heavy rope were filled on the ship, each net holding a full load for a "duck" or a truck of equal capacity. The ship's crane hooked on to the four corners of the net and set the whole thing, net and all, in the body of a waiting "duck." The "duck" at once took off in its character of boat and made for the shore. There it took to its wheels, ran up the beach and to a line of waiting trucks. Here another crane lifted the filled net and lowered it into the truck. Then two corners of the net were detached from the crane hook, the crane started hoisting and the net was pulled out, leaving the cargo in the truck, which set off at once for a supply dump near the front while the "duck" returned to the ship.

In making inspection trips around the Cotentin Peninsula we had to be extremely careful, constantly on guard against mines and booby traps. They were everywhere and caused many casualties. In one location, near the topmost forts on the hill, above Cherbourg, there were so many mines that the bodies of a number of Germans were left lying rather than subject American soldiers to the peril of removing them.

In this sector the Germans had honeycombed the solid rock with strong points, making a miniature Gibraltar. Everything was smashed. Breeches of the enemy guns were blown off by the Heinies before they surrendered, and German clothing, food and equipment were scattered everywhere, either left by the fleeing Germans or captured by our own soldiers as, by brute force, they took one after another of the underground bastions.

As Third Army troops continued to pour across the Channel it became more difficult to place units so that those which were to be committed to the fight first could get out first without, in their dash to the front, crossing the traffic lines of those still coming in.

We all knew the big day was approaching rapidly, and hourly we became more restless. We had been highly trained to be mobile in mind and body—ready to move in any direction at a moment's notice, and the great day, the greatest moment in history for us, was drawing near. We chafed and fretted to go.

5

The Breakthrough

ON 25 July, although Headquarters Third U. S. Army had not become "operational," General Patton was designated by General Bradley as Deputy Commander of all American Troops on the Continent at that time. In this way he took direct command of the VII and VIII Corps for the breakthrough.

Plans for the operation had been in the making in General Bradley's Staff and in our Third Army G-3 Operations tent for weeks. General Patton himself worked out the details making changes daily on our operations map so that everything would be in perfect order for the jump off. It was during these weeks of planning and preparation that General Maddox, our G-3, instructed me as to the tactical plan and advised me of the wishes of General Patton in regard to committing the various divisions and other units to the front lines. As mentioned in chapter three, all Third Army units had to be placed in fields, orchards and woods, in conformity with this tactical plan so as to permit the uninterrupted flow of various types of troops into the breakthrough.

In executing the breakthrough, Patton used not only First Army troops but also a number of his own Third Army units, i. e. the 4th and 6th Armored Divisions, to make the actual breach.

The attack was to commence on 26 July. The code name for the breakthrough operation was COBRA. Two armored thrusts were projected on our operations map, starting from the vicinity of St. Lo, one going in a southwesterly direction toward the important road junction of Coutances, the other going farther south toward Granville, a town on the west coast of the Cotentin peninsula.

The two thrusts were shown on our big map in red lines with arrows at the ends, so that they looked like the fangs of a snake. Operation COBRA was well named.

The three factors in a successful attack in warfare are surprise, speed and firepower. All are necessary. Our higher command had magnificently worked out the over-all strategy for this decisive operation, as will be pointed out later, and the ground tactics were superbly carried out by General Patton and his troops. General Omar N. Bradley was in command of all American forces on the continent at this time and deserves great credit for overall planning and he also showed superb judgment in placing the fiery Patton in charge of the breakthrough itself.

The British, who were fairly heavily weighted with armor and were being reinforced with Canadians in the eastern sector of the Normandy front, were throwing everything they had at the Germans near the ancient city of Caen. Their armor and reinforcements were building up in the rear and it seemed the most natural thing in the world that the breakthrough would be attempted in the east, where the distance to Paris was the shortest and where, if the penetration was successful, the Germans would be split in two.

The Germans clearly feared an armored attack in this sector, up the Orne Valley, for they moved their 5th SS Panzer Division and a battle group up east of the Orne.

The story can now be told how, in the over-all plan, everything was done to make the Germans think this armored attack really was coming in the east, in the British and Canadian sector.

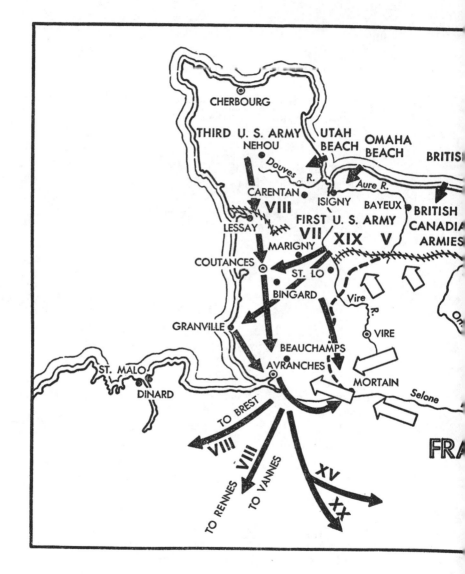

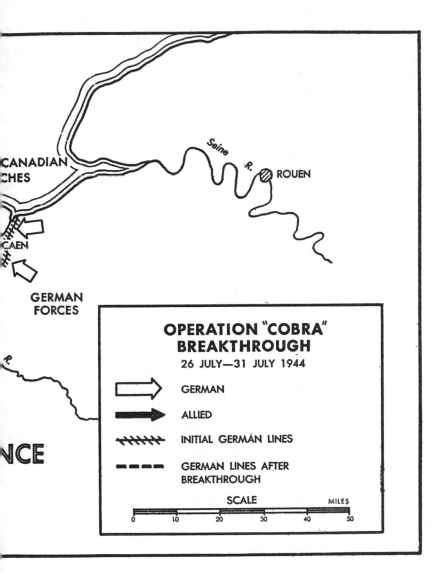

CANADIAN
~HES

CAEN

GERMAN
FORCES

ROUEN

Seine R.

R.

NCE

OPERATION "COBRA"
BREAKTHROUGH
26 JULY—31 JULY 1944

GERMAN

ALLIED

INITIAL GERMAN LINES

GERMAN LINES AFTER
BREAKTHROUGH

SCALE   MILES

0   10   20   30   40   50

Besides the normal build-up in this area, a group of "Special Troops" was brought in behind the lines. They were comparatively few in numbers, but they brought with them all sorts of trick equipment. This included large rubber devices which, when inflated with air, looked like tanks and big guns. Deflated, they were moved in at night, then inflated and partially camouflaged, so that at a short distance they looked like the real thing.

These "Special Troops" also were furnished with complete radio equipment for several headquarters, which they operated cautiously, as would be normal with a headquarters that close to the front. The codes they used, however, were ones we felt sure the Germans could break.

They also had a number of sound trucks, and at night they moved these up to various points closer to the front, where they played phonograph records of the sounds made by tanks and armored vehicles and big guns moving along the roads. The records of the actual sounds had been made during training of armored units back at Forts Knox and Bragg in the United States. With the sound amplified just enough, from a little distance behind the lines and intermingled with the usual racket of night firing, they convinced the Germans we were assembling there for an attack.

Then, in the daylight, when enemy planes came over to investigate, they spotted the increased number of camouflaged vehicles. Also any spies who might have penetrated our lines must have spotted the rubber guns and tanks as genuine and so reported.

Kesselring and von Rundstedt and most of the other high officers of the German command, when interrogated after their capture or surrender, were practically unanimous in saying that our attack, when it came, was not expected in the west of Normandy but in the east.

But in addition to the deception as to where his blow

was to fall, General Patton had another surprise in store. Much has been written about the famous hedgerows of Normandy and the difficulty of fighting among them. These hedgerows are earthen banks which surround each field instead of fences. The fields themselves are small and the dirt banks vary in size, of course, but are from four to six feet high and from three to four feet thick at the base, tapering to a foot or 18 inches at the top. They have been there for generations and are covered with growing bushes and flowers. In many places trees, from saplings an inch or two in diameter to others as thick through as nine or ten inches, grow on the tops.

Each field normally has only one entrance through the dirt wall, with removable rails across it, and between many of the fields run dirt lanes, so that one can travel from one section to another without being seen. The concealment was almost perfect.

Obviously the defender of these hedgerows had an enormous advantage over an attacker. The Germans could conceal their machineguns or tanks behind a hedgerow and as our infantry swarmed over the top or laboriously dug through a section they become easy targets for the waiting guns. Fighting here was reminiscent of trench warfare in World War I, and the hedgerows and lanes became a continuous network of trenches already constructed for the Germans.

The fighting was fierce and deadly. Something had to be done. Many things were tried. American troops had used the tractor bulldozers which accompanied most units, with some success, but they were vulnerable targets. Then bulldozer shovels were riveted on the fronts of tanks. The First Army used these with some success, but they were too slow in getting through. Usually two or three thrusts were necessary to make an opening. Also, bulldozer shovels were rather scarce.

Then someone suggested making hundreds of hedgecutters from the steel of German barricades which had been placed in the sand along all the beaches of Normandy to puncture and wreck our landing craft. This steel, of which the Germans had kindly left an unlimited supply, was just the right type and weight—from a quarter to about a half inch thick and from four to five inches wide, some flat and some angle and T-iron. General Patton took up the idea immediately and ordered every ordnance unit in the Third Army to turn out these hedgecutters by the hundreds.

They were simple in design, rather small in size, and weighed only about 25 or 30 pounds each. They were made of a cutting piece of steel about three feet long, sharpened on the front edge. Near each end of this cutter was welded a piece of heavy angle iron, sharpened at the front. The points extended about six inches in front of the cutter and the square end 12 inches to the rear. These square ends were bolted to the frames of the medium and light tanks. Some play was allowed in the bolt holes, so that the hedgecutter could move up and down and would not break off if a heavy tree stump or rock were encountered.

These cutters struck the earth hedgerows about two to two-and-a-half feet above the surface of the ground, and just above the thickest part of the wall. With one lunge a hole was cut right through the bank and the tank kept going.

I was on an inspection tour of the ordnance units welding these cutters in the field and I saw the demonstration for General Patton. We stood on the far side of a hedgerow and could hear the tank start but could not see it or tell where it was going to strike. Suddenly it crashed through like a bull elephant directly where a ten-inch-thick tree grew in the bank. The tree was knocked to one side, dirt flew in every direction and, without stopping, the tank lunged through and right past where we were standing. Then it turned sharply to the left and crashed through another hedgerow.

It was an inspiring sight. General Patton was delighted and ordered full speed ahead on the welding job so that every fifth tank would have a hedgecutter bolted to its front.

The morning of 26 July, the day that COBRA was to strike, dawned bright and clear. Only a few fleecy white clouds appeared in the sky.

For the first time in history, our High Command had decided to employ heavy bombers in direct support of our ground troops to assist in the breakthrough. More than 3,000 heavy and light bombers of the Eighth and Ninth Air Force were used and 6,000 tons of bombs were dropped preceding the ground attack.

Wave after wave of silvery planes streaked across the sky. It was a wonderful sight. From 1100 until about 1230 death and destruction blasted them from above.

A prominent road in enemy territory had been assigned as the "bomb line", to the north of which no bombs were to be dropped. The U. S. infantry in the front lines had been pulled back a short time before the scheduled bombing to what was thought to be a safe distance—several thousand feet.

Unfortunately, three "shorts" fell among our own troops. The 9th Division reported 33 Americans killed by our own bombs. Major General Manton S. Eddy, commanding the division and who later commanded the XII Corps, said, however, that despite our losses the Air Force had done an excellent job, and later he called for more bombing to assist the attack.

In the 30th Division 130 were killed by our bombs, and Lieutenant General Lesley J. McNair, Chief of Army Ground Forces, observing from our front lines, also was killed.

The cause of these tragic mishaps actually was an errant south wind. It blew the smoke and dust from the first bursts back over our lines. As other bombers came over they bombed the forward edge of the smoke line.

It was reported that the Germans, anticipating an air attack, had dug themselves in and had assembled a large amount of ack-ack to oppose it. The flack was heavy. But they never dreamed of the weight and power of the attack, and they were dazed, stunned and ill-prepared for the heavy armored attack which followed.

The VII Corps, First Army, assisted by the VIII Corps which, as mentioned, had been attached for operations, made the breakthrough. The 2d and 3d Armored Divisions spearheaded the attack. Two days later, 28 July, these forces were augmented by the 4th and 6th Armored Divisions. Four infantry divisions also were employed, the 1st, 8th, 30th and 90th. The total number of Allied divisions ashore in France at that time was 32.

American tanks of the 2d and 3d Armored Divisions smashed a wedge five miles wide into the German defenses west of St. Lo. They captured the town of Merigny, on the road leading from St. Lo to the big road center of Coutances.

In the late afternoon of 26 July I flew back and forth along the front, across the Normandy peninsula, in an L-5 "hedgehopper" plane piloted by Colonel Frank Miller, our Liaison Officer from the Ninth Air Force. From the air we could see clearly the clouds of dust and smoke caused by the armored columns spearheading the attack as they rolled along the roads and lanes or charged through the hedgerows like bulls on a rampage. It was a spectacular sight.

By directing his attack toward the southwest, where it was to be least expected, rather than toward the logical east or southeast, General Patton had caught the enemy off balance. He could not reinforce against the breakthrough, as all his reserves were in the east to guard against the obvious point of attack. The breakthrough plan called for the two columns, after reaching Coutances and Granville, to slice south and slightly east, but still along the coast to Avranches.

Our G-2 Intelligence had led us to believe that there was only a hard crust of German defense in this sector, and that if this could be punctured so we could break out into the open country beyond, in all probability we would be able to play havoc with the enemy supply installations and the groups of German reserves scattered through the territory. This estimate of the situation proved to be good.

On 27 July the VIII Corps took the town of Lessay. On 28 July the 3d Armored Division reached Coutances and the 4th Armored Division, fresh and just recently committed, reached a point several miles below Coutances. On 29 July a new infantry division, the 28th, which had just arrived from England, was assigned to the XIX Corps of the First Army and entered the line on the east. In this way, continual heavy pressure was brought to bear on the German lines farther east to prevent them from reinforcing in the west.

The terrain in the vicinity of Avranches is rough and rugged, bisected by the Selone river. At low tide the stream is only about 20 feet wide, but when the tide comes in it spreads out to 240 feet. Several miles inland along the river are two large dams which create extensive lakes, or reservoirs.

G-2 had learned that the Germans had prepared these dams for demolition. If they should be blown, the whole countryside would be flooded and we might be delayed for days or weeks. This was a truly dangerous threat, particularly if part of our forces should get through into the country below the river and then be cut off where they could not be supplied or reinforced. Throughout this region also spread the inevitable earth hedgerows.

By 1 August the 4th Armored Division had reached the bridges at Avranches and had crossed over. Their speed had been so great that the bridges were taken intact. The 6th Armored had cleared the town of Granville and approached Avranches.

The great speed and diversity of the attack had caught thousands of German troops who had been trying to withdraw south of Avranches. They were either killed, captured or routed.

I saw literally hundreds of their vehicles, both horse-drawn and motorized, which had been smashed to pieces by our combined air and armored assault in the vicinity of Avranches. The litter so filled the roads that bulldozers were sent as quickly as possible to push the dead horses, the wreckage and even the bodies of the Germans out of the way to clear a passage for our troops.

Bands of disorganized Germans still were roaming the countryside, trying to get to the east to rejoin their own forces, and American tanks roved the side roads shooting them up. You never were sure whether you were going to run into our own troops or Germans. During a period of 24 to 48 hours the 4th Armored Division alone reported 4,600 Germans killed.

After crossing the Selone river at Avranches, the 4th Armored was ordered to turn east to secure the dams and other crossings. They moved so rapidly that the Germans had no time to blow the dams.

At 1200 of 1 August, the Third United States Army became "operational", as did the XIX Tactical Air Force, which was to support us. Brigadier General O. P. Weyland commanded the XIX Tactical Air and was, of course, on General Patton's staff. That same day Headquarters of the Third Army moved from Nehou to Bingard, southeast of Coutances.

I shall never forget that day. The excitement was

38

terrific, but everything about headquarters was, as always, calm, purposeful and orderly. We had not seen General Patton for several days, as he had been directing the breakthrough, but now he was in our midst again. The sight of him was wonderful as he strode about, all polished and immaculate. He was in his element and at his best, sure of every move and supremely confident. He reminded one of a magnificent game cock which has just knocked out one adversary and is ready to tackle the next.

We had a short staff meeting of section chiefs in our new location and General Patton addressed us. He said:

"Gentlemen, today we are at the crossroads. Great events are impending and forces are about to be unleashed which may bring about the end of the war even earlier than many think."

Next day our headquarters moved again, to Beauchamps, just north of Avranches and directly in the narrowest part of the breakthrough area. General Patton chose to be there so that he could supervise pushing all his corps and divisions through the approximately eight-mile-wide gap and he wanted his staff with him.

While we were here the Germans, in an effort to close the gap and cut off our troops which were already below Avranches, started a heavy counter-attack toward the west in the vicinity of Mortain with four armored divisions. It was a tense and anxious time. The German attack at first gained ground and captured Mortain. Their planes, all during this period, were out night and day, bombing bridges, troop concentrations and supply dumps in the vicinity of Avranches, and strafing our troops.

General Patton, however, had foreseen this, and while his 4th Armored Division and the 79th Infantry Division and separate tank destroyer battalions battered the German armor from south of Mortain, a fresh infantry division, the 35th, and its tank destroyer battalions pressed down from the north and attacked the flank of the German counter-attack from that side.

It was close for a while as the battle raged back and forth around Mortain. Gradually, after several days, the German spearhead was blunted and finally its force was spent and the Avranches gap was safe.

And all this time, while the crucial battle at Mortain was raging, the "Old Man" never stopped the flow of his armor and infantry through the opening.

The VIII Corps was the first to go through. It had been ordered to turn west toward the port of Brest, at the western tip of the Brittany peninsula.

Other units, then attached to VIII Corps, but later under XII Corps, had gone through with orders to move south through Rennes to Vannes, on the southern coast, to sever the Brittany peninsula from the rest of France.

The XV Corps had gone through under orders to go east through Fougeres and Mayenne.

The XX Corps had gone through to strike southeast through Laval and in a general direction southeast of Paris.

The magnificent American forces had opened a hole in the German defenses. Patton and his Third Army were loose in the open country, about to make the greatest dash in military history, a feat which was to thrill all the people of the free world!

6

Across France—The Bomb Explodes

I N these pages I am trying to do two things—first, to give
any possible military readers a broad picture of the
Third Army situation as it looked at Headquarters from
day to day, and second, to give the non-military reader
some idea of what went on in the Third Army area in
those wild summer days of 1944.

It is impossible for the writer, from his staff experience, to get down into the front lines and describe
much of the daily life and experiences of the hardy infantrymen and tankers who slugged it out with one of the
finest armies the world has ever seen, and by sheer courage,
initiative, hardihood and devotion, administered one of
the most complete and crushing defeats in military history.

I shall, however, illumine the account with incidents and
details that came under my personal observation which
may convey to the lay readers something of the atmosphere
in which their men lived and fought and won—and many
died.

When General Patton hurled the thunderbolt of his
Third Army through the famous Avranches Gap on 1
August, it was composed of four corps—the VIII, which
had reverted to it from the First Army, the XII, the XV
and the XX.

VIII Corps was composed of the 6th Armored and the
8th and 83d Infantry Divisions.

XII Corps was composed of the 4th Armored and the
80th Infantry Divisions.

XV Corps was composed of the 5th Armored, the 79th and 90th Infantry Divisions and the French 2d Armored Division.

XX Corps was composed of the 7th Armored and the 5th and 35th Infantry Divisions.

Thus General Patton had a total of 12 divisions; five armored and seven infantry. Not all went through the eight-mile-wide gap at Avranches in the first few days of August. Two or three of the divisions had not yet arrived on the continent from England or at least were only partially unloaded from the ships, but most of them went through immediately following the great breakthrough and the others followed as fast as they were unloaded and brought up.

Besides the 12 divisions listed, the Third Army also had assigned corps and Army artillery of all calibers, Tank Destroyer, Engineer, Ordnance, Signal, Quartermaster and Medical Battalions, plus the 2d, 15th and 106th Mechanized Cavalry Groups.

Altogether, the total number of troops then assigned to the Third Army was approximately 325,000.

The 4th, 6th and 5th Armored Divisions passed through the gap in that order and spearheaded the drives which now began.

After passing Avranches, the VIII Corps, with the 6th Armored Division in the lead, and the motorized infantry of the 8th and 83d Divisions right behind, was ordered to turn directly west through Brittany and head for the great port of Brest, where so many American troops landed in World War I.

It was also at this time that General Patton ordered organization of a task force made up of mechanized cavalry, tank and tank destroyer battalions, motorized infantry, engineers and other elements necessary for such a force. Brigadier General H. L. Earnest, commander of the 1st

Tank Destroyer Brigade, was placed in command of the task force, with orders to pass over the bridges and through Avranches as rapidly as possible and turning west on the coast road along the north of the Brittany peninsula, to capture all the small towns and ports on the way.

The idea behind this was not merely to seize these towns, but to protect the north flank by preventing the Germans from bringing over from Jersey and Guernsey, the Channel Islands, the division or more they had in garrison there. Task Force Earnest was assigned, of course, to the VIII Corps.

General Patton's instructions to General Middleton, VIII Corps commander, were for the advance guard of each column to surround and contain any enemy groups or strongly defended points encountered and to cut their communications and supply lines; then to form a new advance guard immediately from the main body of the column, which would then by-pass these strong points or enemy groups and advance west as fast as possible, leaving the original advance guard to its task of containing the enemy already encountered. The same procedure was to be followed with each strong point encountered. Thus the main objective was attained with topmost speed.

Although there were, in total numbers, more enemy troops in the Brittany peninsula, including the many ports, than there were in the whole attacking U. S. VIII Corps, the speed of our advance and the maneuverability of our forces left the Germans bewildered, never sure just where we were. As a result they were divided into isolated groups, surrounded, their supplies and communications cut off, and gradually were forced to succumb one by one or were left to "wither on the vine". Later they were either killed by the French Maquis or had to surrender to these French patriot forces.

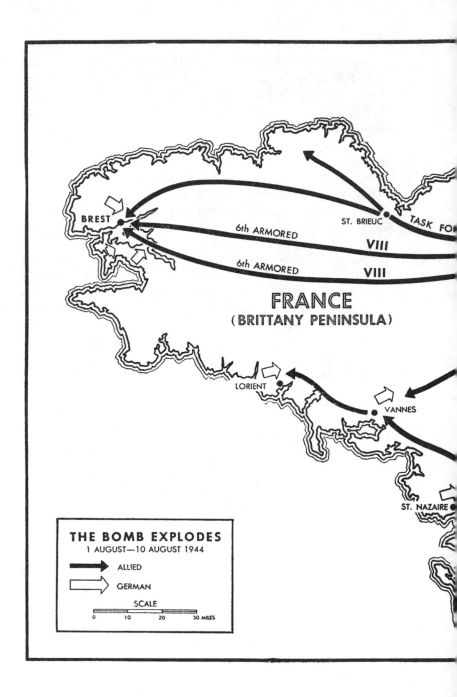

BREST

ST. BRIEUC

TASK FO

6th ARMORED

VIII

6th ARMORED

VIII

FRANCE
(BRITTANY PENINSULA)

LORIENT

VANNES

ST. NAZAIRE

THE BOMB EXPLODES
1 AUGUST—10 AUGUST 1944

ALLIED

GERMAN

SCALE

0   10   20   30 MILES

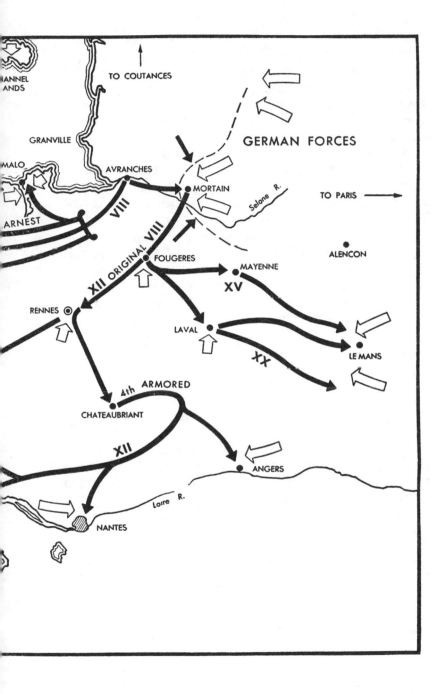

TO COUTANCES

CHANNEL ISLANDS

GERMAN FORCES

GRANVILLE

MALO

AVRANCHES

MORTAIN

Selone R.

TO PARIS

ARNEST

VIII

ALENCON

XII ORIGINAL VIII

FOUGERES

MAYENNE

XV

RENNES

LAVAL

LE MANS

XX

4th ARMORED

CHATEAUBRIANT

XII

ANGERS

Loire R.

NANTES

While the VIII Corps was dashing west in three columns over the main roads of Brittany, the XII Corps spearheaded by the 4th Armored Division, which had turned east after crossing the Selone River at Avranches to secure the river dams and other crossings, now headed due south toward Rennes. Orders were for the armor to surround Rennes, ancient capital of Brittany and filled with people still wearing the black costumes and white lace collars familiar to American tourists before the war, and to allow the accompanying infantry to capture the city and take the German garrison prisoners or kill them.

So fast did our troops move that the 4th Armored Division got south of Rennes almost before Headquarters realized it and Major General John S. Wood, its commander, always an intrepid and dashing fighter, got his columns headed east in the direction of Paris. This was not according to General Patton's plans and a special courier, Major John F. Wolf, was dispatched to Corps with strict orders for the 4th Armored to continue southwest to St. Nazaire, Vannes and Lorient.

The 4th was already beyond Chateaubriant on the road east and had to make a complete half-circle to head west and southwest once more in compliance with these orders.

While the 4th Armored was surrounding the cities on the southern coast of Brittany and capturing Nantes and Angers along the River Loire, the XV Corps, spearheaded by the 5th Armored Division and the 79th Infantry Division, motorized, was dashing east and capturing Fougeres, Laval, Mayenne and Alencon.

Then the XX Corps came through the gap with the 2d French Armored Division and the 5th and 35th U. S. Infantry Divisions and followed closely behind the XV.

It was becoming more difficult each day for our Air

Force to be sure of the identity of columns moving along the roads. Our lines had become so extended that in many instances German columns were found in the rear of ours. It was an extremely fluid situation.

At one time a German column was moving along a road and on almost parallel roads some distance away on each side were American columns. But in that case the airmen had a telltale "fix" on the Germans. There were horse-drawn vehicles in that center column and there wasn't a single horse in the whole American Army in Europe. So the planes came down low and had a field day over the German column, destroying 17 motor and four horse-drawn vehicles.

Of course we could not run the risk of having our own columns shot up by our airmen, so a method was devised to safeguard against that. Panels of fluorescent cloth were provided for attaching to the tops of all our vehicles. They were about four or five feet wide and six or eight feet long and came in two brilliant red and yellow colors, the most easily distinguishable from the air.

Each day an order was issued to all elements, including the Air, specifying the "color of the day"—that is, which color was to be displayed on all vehicles that day, so that our own vehicles could be spotted and there was small chance of the Germans making use of the same scheme to protect their own columns because they could never be sure which color was to be shown.

As a result of this, the Air Forces began reporting the panels an excellent identification, which had eliminated most of their earlier worries about bombing our own columns.

One day, in a wood just north of Fougeres, where Third Army Headquarters had been set up for a short stay, we were all moving toward breakfast under our large, well-camouflaged "circus tent". It was just about 0700 when a plane was heard circling overhead. Suddenly a burst of

50-caliber machinegun bullets came whistling through the trees directly at us.

We leaped behind tree trunks and crouched there until the plane passed. Then, peering through the tree branches, we saw that it was an American single-engined plane. We felt sure it was one the Germans had captured and were using against us, as they sometimes did. We started again through the woods to breakfast, when we heard the same plane overhead, and again a burst of 50-caliber rattled through the trees.

This time our antiaircraft gunners, feeling sure it was a German-manned plane, even though one of ours, opened up on it and in a few moments it was crashing to earth.

Several of us hopped in jeeps and set off in the direction of the crash. We finally found the wreckage and were shocked to discover the body of a young—very young—American pilot of the Eighth Air Force. Undoubtedly he had mistaken our headquarters for a German layout and had thought he was doing his duty in shooting it up.

During these combined drives, air cooperation with the ground forces was closer than ever and the air cover provided by the XIX Tactical Air Command was well-nigh perfect.

During these days the Maquis, or F. F. I. (French Forces of the Interior), which had been the French Underground, were of great help to us in blowing bridges and dynamiting tunnels behind the German lines and otherwise sabotaging the enemy's efforts to bring up reinforcements. They also gave us valuable information of German activities and intentions, locations of reinforcements, troop concentrations and other important information.

An American paratrooper who, in the first days of the invasion, had been dropped in the Rheims area, far behind the German lines, escaped and reported to us. He understood German, spoke it fluently and had lived for several days among the enemy. He reported that even at that early date, 5 August, the Germans were placing five Gestapo and 20 SS men in each German company. Theoretically, of course, this was to stiffen the morale, but actually they were to force the common German soldiers to continue the fight and to shoot them down if they weakened and tried to quit.

It was at this time, also, that Hitler announced another great "purge" in the German army. He named over the radio the first victim to be killed and said the list included four generals and a field marshal.

By 6 August our armored forces had reached a point 30 miles from St. Nazaire, the great German submarine base on the southern coast of Brittany. At the same time our tanks were nine miles north of Lorient, another U-boat base. That same day Royal Air Force Lancasters dropped 12,000-pound bombs on the U-boat base there.

Another Third Army armored column had reached the River Loire at Nantes. Still another column, the XV Corps, had advanced 25 miles east of Fougeres and was now across the wide plain leading toward Paris. There was open country ahead!

General Patton's Third Army thrusts seemed to have disorganized the Germans completely. The VIII Corps in Brittany had made 200 miles in less than a week in its advance from Coutances toward Brest, and had smashed everything before it.

Just at this time a report from the Spanish frontier said that the Germans had begun to move their forces out of southwestern France and along the Mediterranean to reinforce the north or to attack our southern flank.

The American First Army and the British Second Army in those days continued to bring pressure from the north against the German Seventh Army in Normandy and on 6

August British naval forces destroyed a German convoy of seven ships off Brest. All of this showed the magnificent teamwork among the Allies as they destroyed the German war machine.

On 7 Auguest, at the 0900 staff meeting at Third Army Headquarters, General Patton introduced Lieutenant Colonel Coffee, an airman who had bailed out near Angers about five weeks before. He had just gotten back through the lines with the help of French resistance groups. He reported that there were about 300 Germans in Angers; that the German army was methodically retreating east, rolling up its telephone wire as it went, with no excitement and in a very orderly manner; that there were small groups of the enemy in many places, but no large concentrations, and that the bridges at Angers and Nantes were still intact.

As a result of this report, General Patton had decided to send out at once a number of flying combat teams to these areas along the Loire to seize the bridges; he had, in fact, started some of the teams already, before the staff meeting.

By 9 August, Task Force Earnest, of the VIII Corps, had contained all the ports along the north coast of Brittany and on 10 August St. Malo, toughest nut of all to crack, was captured by the 83d Infantry Division, except for the citadel, which held out until 18 August.

On 9 August also the 6th Armored Division was in the outskirts of Brest. At 1500, Major General Grow, commanding the 6th, sent an ultimatum into the city demanding immediate surrender, which was, however, rejected.

The German radio, picked up at our headquarters on 9 August reported that the Third U. S. Army had been identified in Brittany and that the Americans had suffered heavy losses in their operations. No announcement had as yet been made from any Allied source that the Third Army even had become operational.

On 9 August also the XV Corps launched an attack on Le Mans. At 0800 the 2d French Armored and our 90th Infantry Divisions attacked on the left to the north of Le Mans, while the 5th Armored and the 79th Infantry Divisions struck on the right, south and southeast of the city. One battalion of each infantry division was motorized to keep pace with the armor.

On this day I made a trip to contact one of the front line divisions attacking northeast of Le Mans. I started early in the morning, as there was much traffic on the roads and a long distance to travel to get to the head of the column. I arrived at Le Mans just in time to see the 79th Division entering the city. The Germans had pulled out in a hurry.

Most of the city had been cleared and the 79th Infantrymen were walking along each side of the street as they entered. The streets were filled with columns of American motor equipment of all types and descriptions—tanks of the 5th Armored Division, Corps Artillery of all calibers from 105's to 8-inch howitzers, halftracks, bulldozers, tank transporters, and so on.

It was truly an imposing sight. All the town's inhabitants had come out to welcome the American "liberators." They thronged the sidewalks and every window, cheering and waving flags. Men, women and children on the sidewalks were throwing their arms around our soldiers and attempting to hug and kiss them as they strode along with their rifles slung over their shoulders.

The civilians had bottles of wine and cognac which they were trying to give the soldiers, as well as fruit and other food which they attempted to force on our men.

It was a marvelous example of Third Army discipline to see these men trudging along, paying little or no attention to the wonderful reception and the attentions being showered upon them. Any American would have felt pride in our men for the way they conducted themselves in the circumstances and the way they continued to pursue their grim duty of routing the Huns completely from France.

I drove in my jeep in this procession through the streets of Le Mans and finally visited the columns of the 5th Armored Division, which was operating several miles north of the town. The situation at this time was so confused and fluid that you never knew where you were going to contact the enemy. Sometimes he was in front of us, sometimes on the flanks and again units would turn up in our rear. We called it "fighting in Indian country" when conditions were like this, because it was pretty much like what we had read of that sort of thing. It was indeed exciting.

After my visit with two of the combat commands of the 5th Armored, I returned to Le Mans. Being midsummer, the sun was still shining brightly at 7 o'clock and I decided, instead of eating the "K" rations we carried in the jeep, to try to buy a dinner at one of the hotels, as my sergeant driver and I were fairly tired and hungry. The crowds were still milling about the streets and the motor columns were still traveling through toward the front, although the 79th Infantry had all passed through.

We went into one of the big hotels to wash up for dinner and in the washroom I ran into Lieutenant Colonel "Bing" Morris, of our Air Force, and John McVane, a radio announcer, who that night was to make a broadcast over the B.B.C. telling of the advances of the Third Army. Morris, McVane and I decided to have dinner together and we arranged for our drivers to have theirs at a table near us. The hotel was filled with excited French men and women, chattering over the liberation of their city.

We arranged with the manager for the dinner and asked if he had anything good to drink.

"Oui, oui, messieurs," he exclaimed loudly, disappeared from the room and returned in a few minutes with a bottle of Johnny Walker Black Label. It was covered with cobwebs and dust. Presenting it to us, the manager said;

"This, messieurs, in 1939 I hid away in my cellar. I made with myself a resolution. I will not, I told myself, bring this precious bottle forth until the day of victory. This *IS* the day of victory—for Le Mans, mais oui?"

We were enjoying this unexpected treat and responding to toasts of "Vive l'Amerique" by various groups of the French people, and had just finished our soup course. We were about to start the main dinner when there was a terrific burst of gunfire just outside. We dropped our food and rushed to the door, and as we got there we heard the crack of rifles and the crash of broken glass. We could see American soldiers crawling along close to the buildings and firing up at the second and third floor windows of buildings next to the hotel and across the street. French civilians were sprawled in the gutters and against the buildings, seeking shelter.

It appeared that several snipers had been discovered in the upper floors of these buildings and also in a church at the corner of the street. After considerable activity, in which one sniper was killed and another captured, the excitement subsided and we went back to finish our dinner and the Johnny Walker.

7

The Falaise Pocket

TOWARD mid-August, General Patton executed one of those sudden turns for which he was famous and which always threw the Heinies into consternation because they never could forsee or anticipate them.

Instead of pushing his XV Corps on to the east over the open plain southwest of Paris, as must have seemed to the Germans the obvious thing for him to do, he ordered it to thrust directly north toward Alencon, just south of the front in Normandy held by the British and the Canadians.

This movement brought about the famous "Falaise Pocket." The Canadians had driven down from the North and were in the outskirts of Falaise. On 15 August our 2d French Armored Division and the 90th U. S. Infantry Division had reached as far north as Argentan.

At this time the gap had been reduced in width to about twelve miles.

Pressure on the southern flank was continued and on 17 August General Patton completed a regrouping of his forces. The VIII Corps (6th Armored and 8th and 83d Infantry Divisions) was still away in the west besieging Brest.

The XX Corps (7th Armored and 5th Infantry Divisions) was approximately ten miles west of Chartres. Its mission was to secure a bridgehead across the Eure River at Chartres and then await orders.

The XII Corps (4th Armored and 35th Infantry Divisions) was south of Le Mans. It was ordered to attack directly south and capture Orleans on the Loire River.

The XV Corps (5th Armored and 79th Infantry Divisions) was in the neighborhood of Chateauneuf, northwest of Chartres, with orders to push on to Dreux, seize it and then await orders.

General Patton had organized a new Provisional Corps, made up of the 2d French Armored and 90th U. S. Infantry Divisions, from the XV Corps, both now in the vicinity of Argentan, as related, and the 80th Infantry Division, from the XII Corps, which had been moved up to join them. General Patton assigned his own chief of staff, Major General Hugh Gaffey, to command this Provisional Corps and lent him a number of his own officers for a Corps Staff.

His order to General Gaffey was to attack north toward Trun to close the Falaise gap and so to kill or capture the whole German Seventh Army. There wasn't an officer or enlisted man in the Third Army who wasn't confident that this could be done. The Provisional Corps was poised to strike. Canadian armor and infantry were at the town of Falaise and a Canadian Lieutenant Colonel had flown to our headquarters as liaison officer.

Suddenly an order was rushed from higher headquarters to halt the attack of the Provisional Corps. A restraining line was placed along the north of our present position, beyond which we were not to move north. History may one day explain this order more fully.

At all events, the reasons given were that the German forces were to be allowed to pull out to the east through the opening, which by this time had been reduced to only about six or eight miles in width, and were to be strafed from the air.

That is what was done, and while we held to the south, all day long in the brilliant sunshine the German columns

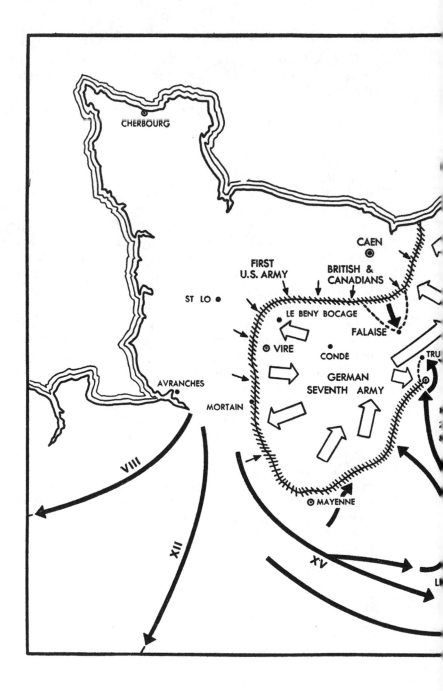

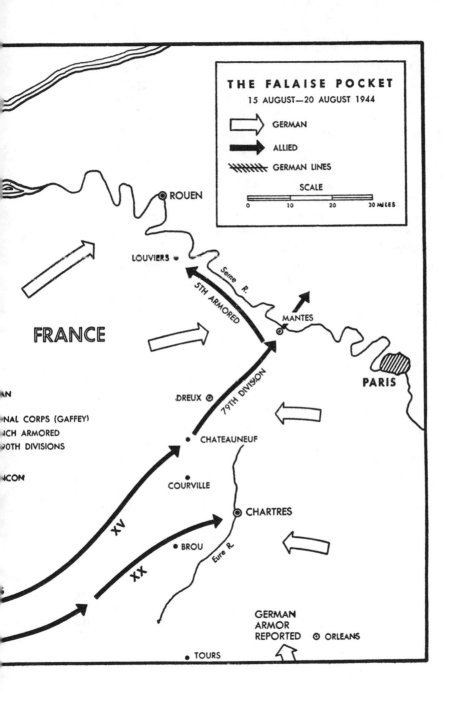

THE FALAISE POCKET

15 AUGUST—20 AUGUST 1944

GERMAN

ALLIED

GERMAN LINES

SCALE

0   10   20   30 MILES

ROUEN

LOUVIERS

Seine R.

5TH ARMORED

MANTES

FRANCE

PARIS

DREUX

79TH DIVISION

AN

NAL CORPS (GAFFEY)
CH ARMORED
0TH DIVISIONS

CHATEAUNEUF

COURVILLE

CON

CHARTRES

XV

BROU

Eure R.

XX

GERMAN
ARMOR
REPORTED   ORLEANS

TOURS

poured east into the heart of France while American Ninth Air Force planes and R.A.F. Typhoons and Spitfires did tremendous slaughter. The roadsides were littered with hundreds of burning, smoking wrecks. At times the skys were so filled with our planes that they criss-crossed and rolled around each other as they jockeyed for position to attack.

A curtain of bombs was laid along the line of German retreat. U. S. Eighth Air Force planes, streaming across the channel from the crack of dawn all through the long summer days, smashed the whole area. In two days alone the Eighth Air Force knocked out five thousand freight cars and attacked more than six hundred locomotives to harry German transport. The Germans fought tenaciously to keep the gap open for their broken and bleeding divisions to escape, while we sat and waited—for a short time.

Perhaps it might be interesting at this point to give a little testimony from the other side, to show what that air attack looked like to the Germans.

Such testimony comes from a General who talked freely to American intelligence officers, after his capture toward the end of the war, perhaps because he felt he had been misused by his superiors.

He was Generallieutnant Fritz Bayerlein, who had been Marshal Rommel's Chief of Staff in Africa. He had been a tank commander and had been assigned the job of organizing and training what the Germans called the Panzer Lehr Division, for the purpose of driving the invading Allies back into the sea.

"We moved as ordered and immediately came under air attack," he said "I lost twenty or thirty vehicles by nightfall. It is hard to remember exact figures for each day, but I do remember very well being strafed personally near Alencon."

"The first air attack came about five-thirty that morning, near Falaise. By noon it was terrible. My men were calling the main road from Vire to Beny-Bocage a fighter-bomber race course—Jabo Rennstrecke.

"They enforced camouflage discipline with a will. Every vehicle was covered with tree branches and moved along hedges and the edges of woods. Road junctions were bombed and a bridge was knocked out at Conde. This didn't stop my tanks, but it hampered other vehicles. By the end of the day I had lost 40 tank trucks carrying fuel and 90 others. Five of my tanks were knocked out, and 84 half-tracks, prime movers and self-propelled guns. My supply echelons were under continual bombardment."

That is one German commander's version.

Although the havoc wrought by the combined air attack was terrific, nevertheless a considerable part of the beaten German forces was able to slip through the trap and escape toward the east, particularly during the hours of darkness.

But General Patton was aiming to knock the German army out of the war, and an order forbidding him to move in one direction was not enough to keep him idle. He had been prevented from closing the Falaise gap and pulling the drawstring on the pocket to capture the whole German Seventh Army, by the order halting him on the Argentan line. But he had not been forbidden to attack to the east or northeast. No wonder the Germans hated and feared him.

Like a champion boxer, he swung a long, looping hook to the northeast along the bank of the Seine River. For this blow he used his XV Corps. Infantry of the 79th Division seized the bridge at Mantes, northwest of Paris, while the 5th Armored Division continued northwest along the Seine, smashing the retreating German armor and infantry just when they had begun to think they were safely away from danger.

The slaughter of the German troops and destruction of their material was tremendous. The pounding from the air and the continuing pressure on the north and west by the Canadians, the British and the American First Army, utterly destroyed a large portion of the German Seventh Army.

At this time several enemy groups were reported by French civilians to be approaching Nantes and Angers from the south. Only the 2d Cavalry (mechanized) was holding Nantes and only one regiment of the 80th Infantry Division had been left to hold Angers.

At Tours there was enemy activity and much mortar fire. An enemy garrison of some 3,000 was reported in Orleans. A group of enemy tanks was reported moving north toward Chartres. This was thought by our G-2 to be part of the 11th Panzer Division, as two soldiers of that division had been taken prisoners by our 7th Armored Division at Chartres.

Elements of the 1st and 12th SS Panzer Divisions were reported in Dreux on 14 August, evidently moving east. Our 7th Armored Division reported that approximately 250 enemy parachutists had been dropped in the vicinity of Courville at 0430 on the 15th, but 35 already had been rounded up and captured.

On 15 August it was officially announced over the American radio for the first time that the Third U. S. Army was operating in France with Lieutenant General George S. Patton, Jr., in command.

While the battle raged in all directions and on all fronts at one time, as we have seen, the Third Army actually had separate corps moving in four different directions at the same time—west, north, east and south.

The Old Man never was perturbed or upset for a moment, however. He was in his glory. He was always confident and assured and maintained confidence always in his staff, his commanders and their troops. The faster things went and the more excitement there was the more he enjoyed it and the calmer he became.

One can realize what a colossal problem our communications and supply had become. Many of our units were operating more than 300 miles from the beaches and our one port, Cherbourg, where our supplies arrived. The SOS (Service of Supply) was amazed, confused and bewildered by the speed of the Third Army, but General Muller, General Patton's G-4 (Supply) performed a masterly job in coordinating them and keeping them informed of the whereabouts of our units even using Third Army trucks to assist the SOS.

Many times he sent our own trucks back all the way to the beaches to bring up supplies. The SOS ran what were called "Red Ball Specials," taking the name from the fast freight specials the railroads ran in the days when our American West was being opened up. These were fast, through truck routes over the main, long-distance highway routes, all the way from the beaches to truckheads up near the front.

Our engineers did an outstanding job, not only bridging the rivers for the advance of our combat troops, but also in repairing the railroad tracks and bridges rapidly, so that in a matter of a very few days provisions were delivered at railheads 30 to 40 miles behind our farthest advances.

The air, too, did its part, not only in air cover and observation, but in flying gasoline to where it was needed, delivering thousands of gallons in 5-gallon cans to airfields directly behind our foremost spearheads. As has been pointed out, the 5-inch asbestos composition pipe lines laid under the English Channel, and over the surface of the ground toward the front, pumped a steady flow of gasoline directly from England, but in the early days the laying of this pipe line could not hope to keep up with the speed of our columns, and without the help of the Air Force the Third Army could not have kept going as long as it did before it had to stop for lack of fuel.

People at home would have been amazed had they seen the vast quantities of fuel necessary to keep our mobile columns and our air fleets in action. It was almost unbelievably stupendous, and the fact that it was produced and delivered to us where and when we needed it as well as it was, speaks volumes for the effort of everyone concerned.

Colonel Hammond, Chief Signal Officer, did a marvelous job in keeping up communications with all of our Corps headquarters. He had his men out day and night in all kinds of weather with the most advanced units, and he connected into all the French commercial communication lines wherever possible. Under the conditions, our phone and radio communications were superb.

There came a time, however, when Third Army Headquarters was in the middle and our Corps, as mentioned before, were going in four different directions and getting farther apart every day. Distances between us and our Corps headquarters ranged from 50 to almost 400 miles as the VIII Corps went west and we went east.

Yet it was absolutely vital that the Old Man have correct and up-to-the-minute information as to our own troop situations and the enemy dispositions on all fronts at all times. Nothing was more important than this, for he must base his decisions, not alone on his own superb judgment, but on the information which he received from subordinate units.

Consequently, during these exciting times, with our Third Army Headquarters moving forward 60 to 80 miles every three or four days and our four Corps headquarters moving every day or two, the problem of liaison and communications became paramount.

Our ground connections, by liaison officers in jeeps, were no longer adequate. Therefore it was decided to have them take to the air and fly back and forth twice a day by plane between Army and Corps Headquarters, and to make daily trips to obtain necessary information from the divisions.

The whole squadron of L-5 planes, 32 in all, belonging to Third Army Headquarters, was placed under the jurisdiction of the Chief Liaison Officer. Three or four planes, or as many as their locations warranted, were assigned temporarily to each Corps for transporting its officers. Information from each Corps about all of its divisions and other units was required to be in our Headquarters twice daily, at 0800 and 1600. The information and reports so brought in were screened and briefed and presented to the General at 0900 at the regular daily staff meeting, and again at 1700.

The rest of the planes in the squadron were used to fly to various divisions for special information, to the rear on supply missions, to higher headquarters, to the other armies on our flanks, or to carry important orders to units. Priorities had to be issued for the use of the planes, but first priority went always to liaison officers to get the up-to-the-minute flow of information from our front line units, which was completely vital and must never fail.

The liaison officers were provided with road maps and they and the pilots were instructed to follow air routes over the main supply roads at altitudes of 500 to 1,000 feet. The roads were fairly easy to follow and also were reasonably well protected by antiaircraft guns on our vehicles and by the many American troop units continually moving to the front. Landings were made in any reasonably level fields near headquarters.

It was around this time that one of our liaison officers to the First Army was shot down in his plane and a machine-gun bullet broke a bone in his forearm.

A Corps liaison officer and his driver, using a jeep before we took to the planes, disappeared entirely while crossing through "Indian country" infested with Heinies. Ten days later their graves were found in a woods, side by side. They had taken the wrong road or had tried to make a short cut.

Another of our Corps liaison officers was driven one night in his jeep off the end of a bridge that had been blown. He and his driver landed 30 feet below on a pile of rocks amid the water. The jeep was wrecked, but the officer and driver, after a few weeks in hospital, returned to work.

Day and night it was necessary to keep the information flowing and many an eerie ride was taken through enemy-infested country or recently liberated French territory which was still dangerous.

I shall never forget one night trip I took, about 110 miles each way, from our Headquarters when it was near Brou, southwest of Chartres, to XV Corps Headquarters near Mantes on the Seine River, northwest of Paris.

The General wanted some special, up-to-date information from all of his units by 0700 the next day. It had to do with the fall of Paris. I dispatched two teams, one of my own officers with a Corps liaison officer, in separate jeeps to the XII and XX Corps. I went myself to the XV Corps. Separate cars were used by each officer, traveling with intervals between, so that if one car was shot up the other might get through. We started shortly before midnight.

What a wild ride it was as we dashed along the lonely roads and through the silent, deserted and partly ruined villages! We traveled with our lights on, although it was against orders. But we were on a special mission, must get back with the information by 0700.

The lights of our jeeps showed up wrecked tanks and dead horses, reminders that war had passed this way. And there were other ghostly sights even more unpleasant. We kept our ears open for unusual sounds and rode with our tommy-guns at the alert. The lights were turned off only when we heard planes overhead, which we feared might be German, but we got back with the needed information at 0645 in the morning, 15 minutes ahead of our deadline.

In the daytime, traveling to the front on various missions, we always carried our tommy-guns at the alert, ready for instant action, and we traveled fast, so as to be a fleeting target. We could observe fairly well on our flanks as we passed open fields, but as we neared a woods in "Indian country" we would look the situation over carefully first, then just as we hit the edge of the woods we would let the jeep out to its maximum speed of 60 miles or more an hour and scamper through the woods like scared jackrabbits, all the time with eyes scanning both sides of the road and "burp" gun or tommy-gun ready.

Many times we came upon tanks, enemy or American, sometimes still burning, other times still smoking from having been afire, with the dead men of their crews strewn around. On one trip, as we went to the front, we came to a great crater which had been blown in the road, apparently by a bomb from one of our own planes. The bombardier obviously had been aiming at a German Tiger tank. The bomb had dropped just in front of the Tiger, for the tank had been wrecked, but its own momentum had carried it down into the crater. An American bulldozer was just starting to push the dirt, thrown out by the explosion, back into the hole.

So great was the speed of our advancing columns that

the bulldozer did not attempt to pull the Tiger tank out, but left it and its dead crew where they were and covered them with earth. That evening as we returned along the same road, one would never have known that anything had happened there as the traffic of war flowed steadily over the new-made, impromptu grave. All was perfectly level and as it had been, except, of course, there was no hard surface at the spot where the crater had been.

Another time, I was returning one night to Headquarters through country over which our armored columns had passed that day. It was about 2250 on a rather lonely back road, and dusk was settling down. Suddenly as we came around a bend in the road, a Heinie tank loomed up in front of us. This one was what was called a Panther tank. Fortunately it was facing the other way and in a moment we realized it was done for, for dead Germans were lying beside it. As we came closer to examine it more carefully we noticed that a short distance off to the left facing down a narrow, dirt lane were four American half tracks, the vehicles which carry the armored infantry of an armored division. They were all perfectly spaced at regular intervals, but they were all stopped. There was a deathly stillness about everything but the half tracks looked as though they were at least partially filled with soldiers. I was curious and got out of my jeep and started toward the first half track. As I got closer I was sure there were men in it, so I turned my flash light on them. There were men in it, but they were dead men, burned to a crisp. Four of them were sitting there, slouched over a little to one side, with their helmets still on their charred heads and their burned hands still clutching their rifles.

I looked in the second half track and three burned bodies were sitting in it. The half tracks were all the same, all four of them. They had the markings of the 4th Armored Division on the vehicles, but what had happened, I will never know. The Panther tank at the bottom of the hill was partly camouflaged with branches of trees. Whether it had surprised them and shot each one as it came down the lane and they finally shot it up, I do not know. It seems more likely that four or more Germans were stationed at intervals behind the hedge along the lane, and at a given signal, they each tossed grenades into one of the half tracks and set it on fire, and most of our boys were killed thus.

8

Paris Falls

WHEN the Third Army burst like a bomb across France in early August, the Germans tried desperately to establish a defense line. They thought that if they could only stop us on some line and compel us to dig in defensively, they could create a system of trench warfare such as that in World War I, and wear us down, making the whole thing so costly to us that in time we would have to agree to a negotiated peace.

But General Patton was not the man to be led into such a disastrous action. He felt, and said: "When you have an adversary staggering and hanging on the ropes, don't let up on him. Keep smashing, keep him off balance and on the run until you have knocked him out completely. That is the way to get this dirty business over quickly and at the smallest cost." And so he kept up the pressure, added to his speed, and never even thought about digging in.

An excellent example of this was the way he committed the 7th Armored Division to battle.

On 14 August it was ordered to attack northeast of LeMans. Its advance elements had landed on the Continent only a few days before. It had traveled steadily from the Normandy beaches and had just started to assemble in its own area the night before it was ordered to attack at 1400 on the 14th.

I conferred with Major General Silvester, the division's

commander, just about the time he was starting his attack. He told me then that part of his division was still on the roads stretching back more than 200 miles to Utah Beach, part of it was unloading on the beaches and some was still on ships crossing the Channel. He was working with only part of his staff and his Chief of Staff had not yet arrived.

I wonder if ever before a division was committed to battle for the first time with its forward elements attacking the enemy and its rear elements still aboard ships more than 200 miles away!

Incidentally, that statement may give lay readers some inkling of the magnitude of an armored division with full battle equipment. It has been estimated that such a division, if in marching order with intervals properly spaced according to regulations and moving on a single road (which would never occur in a battle area), would extend over a road distance of close to 100 miles.

One day we picked up an American glider pilot on the road. Not knowing we were from Third Army Headquarters, he told us:

"I sure would like to meet this General Patton some time. He must be some guy. Do you know that two different times lately we have been ordered to capture German airfields in enemy territory and hold them until his forces arrived. Each time we had been briefed and were all set to take off and each time word came that Patton had already taken the damn fields."

That airman, like the rest of them, had the greatest respect and admiration for General Patton, as he had for them.

One day during August, while these great strides were being made, General Weyland, commanding the XIX Tactical Air Force which supported us, was sitting next but one to General Patton in the daily 0900 staff meeting. Different things had been discussed and one of the air officers was explaining how difficult it was becoming for the Air Force to get its supplies up and to keep up its communications, and even to get suitable airfields from which to support our varied lightning thrusts.

The officer was really making out quite a case for himself and the Air Force, and was almost suggesting that possibly it might be better if things were slowed down a bit. Suddenly General Patton leaned forward to look at General Weyland past his Chief Staff, who sat between them, and said, just loud enough for all of us to hear:

"Opie, it would be a terrible thing if the Ground Forces should outrun the Air Forces, wouldn't it?"

Everybody laughed, including Weyland, and we never heard anything more about the difficulties the air had in keeping up.

As our columns spread through France, the Germans not only could not stop us, they could not even get their own supplies and equipment out of our way. We captured thousands of tons of supplies—food of all descriptions, millions of pounds of frozen meats, canned vegetables and fruits, gasoline, clothing and so on.

Our messes were immediately augmented and for a while we had almost more food than we could eat. Carloads of German fur coats and winter clothing were captured, together with silk and rayon parachutes. Many a soldier mailed home to his girl or his family, boxes filled with such things, especially silk parachutes, from which dresses and scarfs could be made.

Our soldiers didn't think of this stuff as loot. They called it "liberated" material. It had been in possession of the enemy and as such was legitimate spoils of war. There was no means of telling whether the Germans had looted it from the civilian population, or of determining who were the rightful owners if there had been proof that it was German loot.

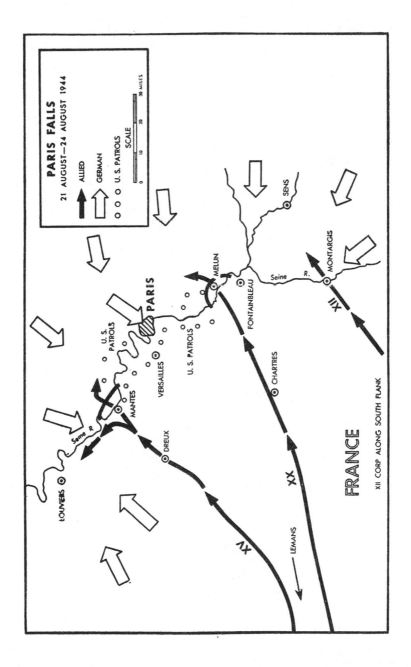

PARIS FALLS
21 AUGUST—24 AUGUST 1944

ALLIED
GERMAN
○ ○ ○ U. S. PATROLS

SCALE
0   10   20   30 MILES

PARIS

U. S.
PATROLS

U. S. PATROLS

VERSAILLES

MELUN

FONTAINBLEAU

Seine   R.

SENS

MONTARGIS

CHARTRES

MANTES

Seine R

DREUX

LOUVIERS

LEMANS

XX

XV

XII

FRANCE

XII CORP ALONG SOUTH FLANK

One of the greatest prizes, from the soldiers' viewpoint, was the whole Wehrmacht winter supply of fine wines and liquors. At Angers we captured 9,000 cases of Cointreau alone. This liqueur and great quantities of wine were stored in warehouses and in some places on airfields, ready to be shipped to Germany. At one airfield it was stacked "seventeen cases high and as far as the eye could see." Among the brands captured were Hennessy and Martell brandies, including the 39-year-old Cordon Bleu and even some Napoleon brandy; D.O.M. Benedictine and the Cointreau already mentioned; Noilly Prat vermouth, various rums and all the finest wines of France, including tens of thousands of cases of the best champagnes—Mumm's, Pommery, Piper-Heidsieck, Cordon Rouge, Moet et Chandon, and so on, and other liquors and cognacs too numerous to mention.

As usual, General Patton was very practical about the whole thing. He felt that our officers and enlisted men should be allowed to share and enjoy some of the spoils they had captured. The only thing he would not stand for was drunkenness. And to the everlasting credit of our men and the superb discipline of the Third Army, there never was any drunkenness, or if there was it was so isolated and restrained that it never was visible and never interfered with our serious duty of pursuing the enemy relentlessly. General Patton just would not tolerate intoxication.

Units were allowed, under the supervision of General Muller, our G-4, to send trucks to cart away the wines and liquors to be distributed among the troops. A drink of cognac was issued before many evening messes and champagne was served at so many noon and evening messes that we soon grew tired of it and said: "Take it away, we prefer water."

Many GI's, while not in the immediate fighting, carried bottles along with them, and units carried large supplies for miles and issued it over the following weeks and even months.

This was one more example of how practical and broad-minded General Patton was about everything. He felt that among all the discomforts of war, to say nothing of the constant danger, a man was entitled to a little cheer as long as he did not abuse the privilege. He believed that every GI was a man and a soldier, fighting for his country and for freedom, and should be treated as a man.

Major George W. Elkins, Jr., an assistant artillery officer of XX Corps, was one day flying over "Indian Country" in a cub plane. Normally the Heinies did not fire on these little observation planes for fear of giving away their positions and bringing down our artillery fire on them. This particular day they did open up, however, and shot one wing off Major Elkins' plane.

The plane carreened toward the earth and landed upside down on top of some thick trees. Fortunately as the plane hit, the engine was torn loose and caught fire on the ground.

German machine guns immediately opened up on the plane and the bullets splattered through the body narrowly missing the Major and the pilot who were strapped in and could scarcely move in their inverted positions.

Two of our light tanks which had witnessed the whole affair, came over and after blasting out the German machine gun nest, called up to the plane to see if either of the occupants was alive. When they found that they were, one tank remained on guard, while the other went to fetch an ambulance.

When the medical men arrived and cut the two men loose they found that they had miraculously escaped. Major Elkins had received a gash on his knee and the pilot had only torn his trousers. Otherwise they were both O. K.

68

And so the Third Army rolled along and the pressure against the Germans rose and our speed increased. The Old Man, however, never lost sight of the first and greatest mission of warfare, "to destroy the enemy in the field." I often thought of this as we passed along and saw the thousands of wrecked German vehicles of all descriptions—tanks, trucks, wagons, staff cars, guns, half-tracks, every sort of vehicle and weapon in the enemy's arsenal, all charred and burned and smashed, lining the roads and scattered through the fields. Here was the wreckage and wastage of war at its worst or, from our standpoint, at its best. It was a sight never to be forgotten, this equipment, the pride of the German army, mired, smashed, burned, irretrievably destroyed by our own columns and the covering air power.

General Patton was not worrying about conquering territory or the fall of cities. He well knew that as his forces destroyed the enemy field army, the territory and the cities would fall of their own accord.

Consequently he threw two prongs, one, the XV Corps, to the northwest of Paris, across the Seine River at Mantes; the other, the XX Corps, to the southwest of the French capital across the Seine at Melun. The German Seventh Army was being cut to pieces in the north and the German First Army was trying desperately to hold the line as we approached Paris from the south.

All during these twin drives, the Third Army was operating with an exposed flank, often 450 miles along the Loire River on the south. The Old Man, however, kept one corps, the XII, composed of the 4th Armored and 35th Infantry Divisions, working along this flank to deal with enemy units piecemeal as they approached from the south. He also relied heavily on the XIX Tactical Air Force to reconnoiter the country to the south and give him ample warning of any serious danger from this source.

On 18 August the B.B.C. reported the American Third Army 30 miles from Paris and almost simultaneously the Germans said it was only 23 miles. Great numbers of barges were reported by our air reconnaissance to be in the Seine River, probably for use by the Germans in an attempted withdrawal to the east.

The population of Paris was warned by radio from SHAEF (Supreme Headquarters, Allied Expeditionary Forces) to be ready to rise against the Germans, but to do nothing until they were given a signal.

On 19 August the Provisional Corps, composed of the 2d French Armored and the American 80th and 90th Infantry Divisions, which General Patton had poised to close the Falaise Pocket but which had been halted by order from higher up, reverted to the First Army.

On 21 August our G-2 furnished an estimate of enemy strength in various sections with which it was conceivable we might have to cope. It was as follows:

East and south of Paris—elements of five divisions with a total strength of approximately 35,000.

North of Dreux and west of the Seine—elements of several divisions totaling about 30,000.

South of the Loire River—approximately 22,000.

In France north of the Seine—75,000.

In Belgium and capable of reaching the area north of the Seine in about three days—19,000.

In Holland and capable of reaching the same area in about five days—23,000.

In Denmark and capable of reaching the same area in about one week—35,000.

In Norway and capable of reaching the same area in about two weeks—75,000.

In Germany and able to arrive in about two weeks—80,000.

This gave the enemy an overall total of 33 divisions, about 307,000 troops.

On this same date, 21 August, it was reported that the population of Paris had risen against the enemy, that rioting had started and that martial law had been invoked. And German reports said the Americans had crossed the Seine and had formed a bridgehead.

Simultaneously the Germans were reported to have organized 20 crossings of the Seine in their efforts to escape. Ironically enough, the barges they were using in this flight from the Allies were those they had built and transported to the Channel coast in 1940 for an invasion of England which never came off.

Third Army troops continued to close in on the French capital and fierce fighting was going ahead on both sides of the Seine near Mantes. Third Army patrols were reported in Versailles, ten miles from the center of Paris. American planes flying over the area saw American armored columns pushing forward so fast that the airmen at first thought they must be the retreating Germans, speeding to get away.

By 21 August, the 79th Infantry Division of our XV Corps had completed its mission of securing the crossing of the Seine at Mantes and had penetrated beyond to a depth of eleven kilometers (nearly seven miles). The 106th Cavalry, reconnoitering to the south, made contact with the 43d Reconnaissance Squadron of the XX Corps, but the 5th Armored Division was meeting the heaviest resistance it yet encountered in its advance along the Seine toward Louviers. There still was fight left in some of the German outfits, and the 5th was attacked on both flanks and was lashed by artillery from across the river.

In parts of the Third Army area a spell of bad weather cut down air activity, but in the XV Corps area the enemy suddenly unleashed a spasm of great activity in the air. German planes swept over the CP (Command Post) of the corps several times. Two of our observation planes were destroyed on the ground and the bridge at the crossing was bombed heavily, but our ack ack knocked down 16 enemy planes in one day.

A crisp summary of the picture in France was given by the British Broadcasting Company's newscast of 22 August, which said:

"American Third Army troops are across the Seine River on both sides of Paris. They have now established a strong bridgehead over the river near Mantes and are threatening the rear of the German forces retreating from Normandy. Canadian, United Kingdom and First U. S. Army forces pursuing the Germans are nearly half way from Caen to the Seine River. South of Paris, more American Third Army forces are reported to have crossed the Seine River near Fontainebleau. Inside Paris, street fighting is reported to be getting fiercer."

Our VIII Corps at this time was preparing for an all-out attack on Brest, having failed to reduce the port by routine siege. The corps had been given the additional mission of protecting all the crossings of the Loire River on the south to a point as far east as Orleans, and elements of its 83d Infantry Division were on guard at Rennes, Nantes, Angers and Orleans.

The famous citadel of St. Malo, on the Brittany peninsula, far to the west of Third Army's eastward plunge, finally surrendered on 18 August. A staff officer who was present at the surrender and later visited the fortress said that one of the reasons for the surrender was a shortage of ammunition. This may have been one reason, but there was a much better story behind what finally caused the citadel's garrison to capitulate.

The true reason they surrendered is that they ran out of water. A few days before the surrender, four enlisted men of the Third Army were taken prisoners in a sortie. One of these American lads was put on KP duty and became friendly with one of the Germans helping in the kitchen. The German at one time had lived in the United States, spoke English, and didn't care for his present associates and surroundings. He and the American together tapped the water supply tanks, letting the precious fluid escape and causing such a shortage that the garrison could hold out no longer.

It was about this time that 16 Napalm, or jelled gasoline bombs were dropped by our airmen on the small island of Zembre, near St. Malo, from which enemy gunfire had been harassing our troops and on which enemy movements had been noted. That ended resistance.

On 22 August our XII Corps was meeting strong resistance from armor, infantry and artillery in the vicinity of Montargis, farther south of Paris.

French civilians reported an enemy force of about 2,000 assembling at Ferrieres. Enemy forces had been observed south of the Loire, southeast of Orleans, with much horse-drawn equipment, indicating an infantry division. Artillery shells were still falling on Orleans. G-2 also reported many other groups south of the Loire, which were thought to be replacement battalions.

We lost the XV Corps from our Third Army when it reverted to the First Army at 0600 on 24 August, but the loss of this great fighting unit was overshadowed by other news that came in later in the day.

Paris had Fallen!

A Provisional Corps formed by the First Army, made up of the 2d French Armored and the 4th Infantry Divisions and the 106th Cavalry, together with some elements from the 21st Army Group (British), entered the French capital and, with the able assistance of French Forces of the Interior within the city, forced some 10,000 of the garrison who had not fled to surrender.

Oddly enough, Marseilles, far to the south, surrendered to the Seventh U. S. Army and the F.F.I. on the same day, the two largest cities of France thus being liberated simultaneously.

And, as if that were not enough good news for the Allied world in one day, Rumania, first of Hitler's satellites to desert the sinking Nazi craft, accepted peace terms. That August day was one of the blackest the Germans had known in the war. Allied troops, ashore on the Continent of Europe just 80 days, already had covered more than half the distance between Cherbourg and the German border.

The bells of Westminster Abbey in London were rung in triumph. In Quebec and Montreal the French-Canadians rejoiced, as indeed did all the people of the whole free world.

Two days after the freeing of Paris, on 26 August, I was returning from a visit to one of our front line units. Since Sergeant Corocci, my jeep driver and a fine fellow, had never been to Paris and was very anxious to visit it—this was the only reason, of course—I decided to make a short detour—only about 60 or 70 miles—to have a first hand glimpse.

As we got into the city's outskirts, we ran into a great crowd, filling the whole of a wide street. They were all watching something going on at a house on one side. Every few minutes there would be loud cheers and shrieks of laughter. I told Sergeant Corocci to pull up along the curb and I pushed my way through the crowd to see what was going on.

Presently I saw. The crowd had rounded up a number of young women, some of them quite young and beautiful, who had fraternized with the German officers.

One at a time, the women were brought forward to the edge of an open veranda on the second floor of a building, so that all could see them. An old, gray-haired

74

woman called something to the crowd for each woman exhibited—probably naming her and telling what she had done in consorting with the enemy. And as she finished, the crowd yelled and booed.

Then the girl would be thrust into a chair and held while hair clippers went quickly about her head, shearing her down to the scalp. Then she was hauled up and again exhibited to the crowd, her head white and nearly bald. Now she looked like a plucked chicken. All this delighted the crowd, which roared its laughter, mingled with loud boos.

Not all the women were cowed, however. One, angry and defiant, managed to snatch an arm free and, while she stuck her tongue out at the crowd simultaneously flipped her thumb and fingers to her nose and gave them a perfect "greetings from Atlantic City." And the crowd enjoyed that, too. It let out a roar of laughter.

As we got farther into the city, we encountered many great log and concrete barriers behind which had been placed machineguns and artillery for German defense of the city. In many streets we saw dozens of German vehicles, wrecked by sabotage of the F.F.I.

Central sections of the city were little damaged by bombs or gunfire. The streets were swarming with people, all cheering, singing and just milling around. There were practically no vehicles except jeeps and other American cars, filled with American and French soldiers. The 2d French Armored Division was there, of course, but it was equipped with all American vehicles, including tanks.

Girls and other civilians were riding the boulevards with soldiers who could not have prevented it if they had wanted to. If you stopped or even slowed your car, civilians swarmed over it and tried to hop aboard. The place was really a madhouse.

We circled around the city for a couple of hours, dodging pedestrians and seeing the famous sights—the

Louvre, the Opera House, the Eiffel Tower, the Cafe de la Paix and the Champs Elysees. As we went around the Arc de Triomphe we passed an American command car (large jeep) with the top down. In it was Captain Hack, who had been with me in my former artillery regiment. I waved at him and he recognized me. I told my driver to pull up along the curb and wait for him. The Captain pulled up a little way behind us and jumped out to come over to me.

Before we could stir, the car was packed solidly, front and back and both sides, with an excited, jabbering crowd. At once the fun started. There were women and girls all over the place. They climbed all over the jeep and us. They grabbed me, hugged and kissed me and tried to pull me from the car. I called to the Sergeant to start the motor and then I saw that he was having the same difficulty I was. He was a big fellow, well over 200 pounds, but the women were lifting him bodily from behind the wheel. By this time we were both fighting desperately these wild, jabbering girls, whose chief intent seemed to be only to express their exuberance and to show gratitude to "les liberateurs". Fortunately, Corocci got one foot on the starter, set the motor going, then gave it a quick shot of gas.

The jeep engine roared and the crowd fell back for a moment, just long enough for us to get started.

As we moved off, I turned to see how my friend, Captain Hack, was making out. There he was, high in the air in the arms of that howling, excited crowd and being carried, I know not where, for I've never seen him since.

We thought we had seen enough of Paris by that time, so we left the city. It was safer out among the Germans.

On the outskirts of the city I came across an old friend, a French Major with the 2d French Armored Division. He had been with me as liaison officer when his division was attached to the Third Army during the breakthrough and until just a week before this meeting.

I said to the Major, who spoke English fluently:

"Congratulations on your liberation of Paris!"

He looked at me quizzically for a moment, trying to determine whether I was being sarcastic. When he realized I was not, he said:

"Thanks, Colonel. But we know, and you know, that we did not liberate Paris. You Americans did that. But it was a wonderful gesture, your letting us enter first, and one which France will never forget."

9

Stopped, But Not by the Germans

THE fall of Paris never halted General Patton and his Third Army for a moment. It was a momentous event in the war, this liberation of the greatest capital held in thrall by the Germans, but the enemy armies were still afield and still to be dealt with, and so our armored columns pressed forward to the east with even greater speed.

The Germans kept up their desperate efforts to dig their heels in some place, come to a halt and force us into static warfare, and many a hot battle resulted when we rushed upon them to keep them in flight. As always, our columns either smashed right through them or, if they were in great strength, by-passed them and left them to be surrounded and mopped up later according to the pattern set for the VIII Corps in its Brittany adventure.

The same litter of smashed and burned tanks, cars and trucks and of dead horses and dead men paved the roads east of Paris as it had to the west. All had to be cleared from the roads as quickly as possible to provide passage for our combat columns, and our Ordnance Units did an outstanding job. In most instances trucks were able to pull the wreckage off the roads, but when it was piled too deep bulldozers were brought up and they made short work of it. Ordnance men had instructions to salvage any German equipment that was still usable, and a considerable amount was put to work for us as a result of their efforts.

It goes without saying that we were not accomplishing all this without sustaining material losses ourselves. Tanks, as well as other vehicles, were smashed and burned, but we always had replacements. Huge tank transporters brought brand new tanks up just behind the front, where they could be taken over by crews and delivered under their own power to the armored divisions that needed replacements. This way our full strength was kept up continuously, or nearly so.

By 28 August our troops were once more moving over historic ground familiar to many of our officers, where the names of towns, villages, woods and rivers were household words in America just 26 years before.

On that date our XX Corps, spearheaded by the 7th Armored Division with the 5th and 9th Infantry Divisions following closely, was advancing toward Chateau-Thierry, one of the first French place names to become familiar to every American in World War I. American troops were fighting again in the Valley of the Marne.

This time, however—although there was bitter fighting in spots and at one point I saw four American tanks knocked out—we did not tarry long. On 29 August the 7th Armored crossed the Marne bridge at Chateau-Thierry and the same day reached the Vesle River in the vicinity of Rheimes.

In a few hours our troops covered more ground than we had covered in the same sector in eight weeks in 1918. As I passed through the region I saw all the little French towns for which we had fought so long and so hard then. They were all in ruins in 1918, but now most of them had not been hurt seriously, as our armored might rolled through after the Heinies. These villages were in far better shape than those of Normandy, where we had been forced to tear the Germans loose to start them running and where most of the towns and villages were left in ruins.

On the hillsides, as we approached the towns of Fismes

79

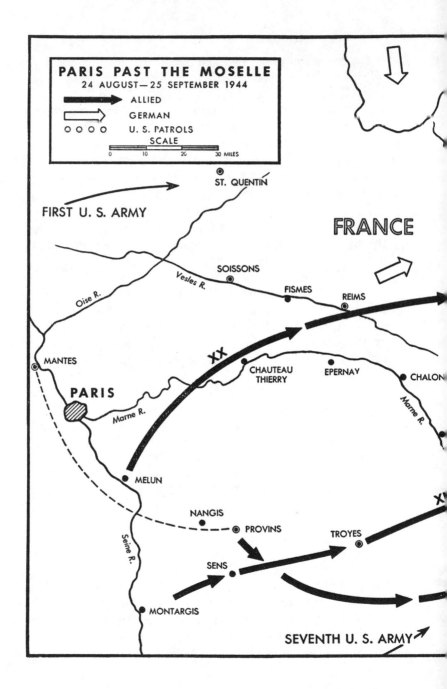

PARIS PAST THE MOSELLE
24 AUGUST—25 SEPTEMBER 1944

ALLIED

GERMAN

U. S. PATROLS

SCALE

0   10   20   30 MILES

ST. QUENTIN

FIRST U. S. ARMY

FRANCE

SOISSONS

Vesles R.

FISMES

REIMS

Oise R.

MANTES

XX

CHAUTEAU
THIERRY

EPERNAY

CHALON

PARIS

Marne R.

Marne R.

MELUN

NANGIS

PROVINS

TROYES

Seine R.

SENS

MONTARGIS

SEVENTH U. S. ARMY

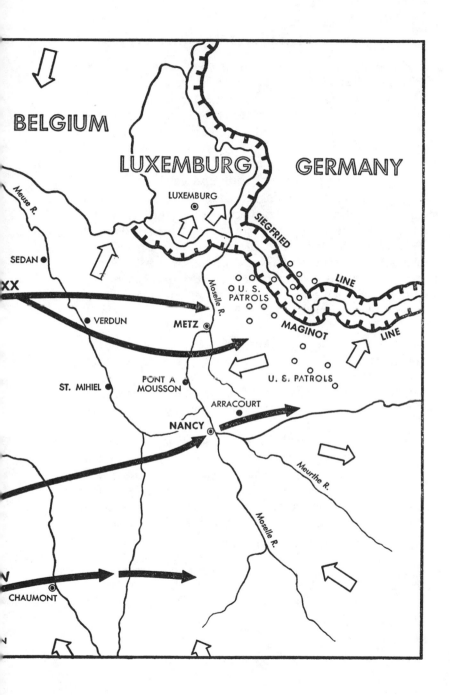

and Fismette, on opposite sides of the Vesle river, many of the foxholes and trenches which were dug in 1918 by the division with which I served, and in which we slept and fought for weeks, were still plainly visible in the hard clay soil—only they weren't called foxholes then. They were called slit trenches. The mere crossing of the river at that point in 1918 turned into a matter of days and was an epic of blood and death and valor.

It gave one an odd feeling to think back over 26 years and to realize that here we were once again, some of us the same men, in exactly the same spot as then and for the same purpose—to drive out the blasted Germans. Surely man should use the brains God gave him to better purpose than repeating every quarter-century the great crime that is war. Surely we must devise some means of preventing another such holocaust.

On this same day, 29 August, we regained our XV Corps, which had been with the First Army only five days.

I have referred several times to the liaison reports and briefing taken at General Patton's daily 0900 staff meetings. Later these notes would be read to the 25-odd liaison officers assembled in the G-3 liaison section of Third Army Headquarters, and the officers would then take off to their own headquarters with the information. With the idea that the reader may be interested in knowing what such a briefing was like, let me here present, as a sample, a verbatim copy of the briefing of 29 August:

S–E–C–R–E–T

```
                              SECRET
Headquarters               AUTH: CG, TUSA
    Third United States Army     INIT: BGW
    G-3 Section (Liaison) DATE: 29 August, 1944
        A P O 403
    Briefing of G-3 Liaison Section and Liaison
Officers
```

STOPPED, BUT NOT BY THE GERMANS

By Colonel Brenton G. Wallace

G-3 Situation as of this morning.
VIII Corps—Situation generally unchanged
The attack on BREST is progressing slowly.
The 6th Armd Div is patrolling in the vicinity
of LORIENT. The 83d Div has units at BREST,
ST. MALO, NANTES and along the line ANGERS-
TOURS-ORLEANS, with the CP at CHATEAUBRIANT.

XII Corps—The 106th Cavalry has now relieved the 2d Cavalry and has been attached to
the 35th Div to assist in patrolling along the
southern border—ORLEANS-TROYES. The 2d
Cavalry is reconnoitering toward the front or
northeast of the XII Corps. VITRY has been
taken by the 4th Armd Div. The 4th Armd is
to attack this morning with the 80th Div toward CHALONS sur Marne.

XX Corps—The 5th Div is along the MARNE
making crossings. The 9th is also crossing
in the direction of RHEIMS. The 7th Armd—All
three combat commands are across the MARNE.
They crossed at CHATEAU-THIERRY and are now
reported along the VESLE River in the vicinity
of RHEIMS.

The nearest point that our troops are to
Germany is now in the neighborhood of VITRY,
which is approximately 100 miles.

There has been a shift in the line between
First and Third U. S. Armies which gives
CHATEAU-THIERRY to the First U. S. Army,
although we still retain the road rights to
cross there.

First Army, VII Corps—The 3d Armd is
approaching SOISSONS, followed by its infantry divisions. V Corps is still in Paris.
XV Corps is scheduled to revert to Third Army
today and is to assemble in the area NANGIS-
PROVINS.

The British are now reported to have closed
in to the west bank of the SEINE and have
made one or two crossings.

AIR—Activity was limited yesterday due to
the weather. Two enemy planes were destroyed
in the air and two on the ground with a loss

81

of two of our own planes. The claims for
yesterday were: 31 locomotives, 81 railroad
cars, 28 tanks, 352 motor cars, 7 guns, all
destroyed; 2 fuel dumps hit, 1 CP bombed,
3 airfields attacked, 7 barges hit.

Today two groups of fighter-bombers will
be over BREST whenever the weather permits.
There will be one fighter group over the XII
Corps and one over the XX Corps, with a third
in reserve. Leaflet missions will be flown
over six or eight towns, which are VERDUN,
RHEIMS, ST. QUENTIN, etc.

G-2—VIII Corps—The enemy is still holding
an island off ST. MALO. It is reported that
400 of the enemy made an attack on a small
town south of REDON in the BRITTANY peninsula
a day or two ago. They captured the town,
took a lot of food supplies with them and re-
tired south of the LOIRE River. The 4th Armd
reports considerable enemy resistance north
and east of VITRY.

PWs and some documents have been captured
within the last day or two from the 15th, 3d
and 90th Panzer Grenadier Divisions. These
divisions were last reported moving from
ITALY. They were all divisions which had
been reconstituted, having been destroyed on
other fronts. The 3d was destroyed at STALIN-
GRAD, later reconstituted and fought in ITALY.
The 90th fought through the desert warfare and
was totally destroyed in TUNISIA. It was reconstituted and again committed in ITALY.
The 15th fought in LIBYA and was also destroyed in TUNISIA.

Civilian reports indicate large enemy
groups in the area south of TROYES down to
DIJON. These reports run as high as 50,000.
Troop movements have been observed by air in
DIJON. The bridges along the MARNE from
CHALONS to VITRY are all reported out, by air.
The CHATEAU-THIERRY bridge was taken intact,
but the bridges from there west along the
MARNE are reported by civilians to have been
mined ready to be blown.

The 7th Armd reported only scattered resistance in its front. There were 300 enemy vehicles observed moving northeast from RHEIMS. Considerable enemy movement has been reported in all sections of the front, moving east and northeast. The 9th Panzer Division, which was in front of the 79th Division in the bridgehead, is reported moving to the northeast. The 79th Division also reports that they have considerable activity from three infantry divisions still in their front.

Higher headquarters report heavy rail movements from the north of FRANCE and the LOW COUNTRIES toward the SOMME River. SS troops have been reported moving toward GERMANY from DENMARK and HOLLAND.

AIR reconnaissance missions will be flown daily by our air forces along the whole length of the LOIRE River and in the whole front of the Third U. S. Army north and east in the direction of VERDUN, METZ and SEDAN.

PWs reported by the Third U. S. Army to date total 68,000; estimated enemy wounded, 57,000; enemy dead, 17,000.

PRESS and RADIO—The last of the Germans in the VERSAILLES area have surrendered. Approximately 5,000 PWs were taken there, making a total on the PARIS area of approximately 17,000.

The RUSSIANS report that the 12 divisions encircled in BESSARABIA have now been annihilated.

In BULGARIA it is reported that the German troops are moving out toward GERMANY.

B. G. W.

S–E–C–R–E–T

From this it will be seen that the whole Third Army got a daily quick resume, not only of the situation affecting its own organizations, and of the enemy, but, so far as it was known, of the other American armies and of our Allies.

That was the roundup of news given our liaison officers for the information of their commanders on 29 August. Three days later, on 1 September, the whole picture had changed again.

The XII Corps reported the 4th Armored Division across the Meuse River and east of St. Mihiel, with the 80th Infantry Division approaching St. Mihiel; the XX Corps reported the 7th Armored and the 5th Infantry Divisions also across the Meuse and east of Verdun, with the 90th Infantry Division at Rheims.

That day was the fifth anniversary of the German invasion of Poland which started the Second World War, and it found the German armies in retreat on every front.

The British were reported in Amiens and mopping up in the Pas de Calais area, destroying the sites from which flying bombs had been launched against England. The American First Army was approaching the Belgian border. The Canadians were in Dieppe and Abbeville, and the Germans began flooding the low sections of Holland and Belgium with the sea.

It was at this time that General Omar N. Bradley, commander of the 12th Army Group, was given a command status equal to that held by General Sir Bernard L. G. Montgomery, but on the same day General Montgomery was elevated to the rank of Field Marshal by King George VI.

And now the Third Army, after taking Verdun, had reached the Moselle, the last big river before Germany, and had crossed over in the vicinity of Nancy and Metz and was approaching the German border. At one point our troops were reported by the Germans to be only eleven miles from the border.

Further indication of the crisis faced by the enemy came in the forenoon of 2 September, when the powerful enemy-controlled radio stations in Brussels and Luxembourg closed down suddenly.

We were so close to Germany now that our air reconnaissance was flown almost entirely over that country, air patrols penetrating the enemy homeland to a depth of 50 miles.

They brought back some amazing reports. They had flown over the Maginot Line at an altitude of 150 feet and because not a shot was fired at them they concluded it was deserted. The German Siegfried Line also, they said, appeared to be neither manned nor gunned. It will be remembered that the Maginot Line had been erected by France along her eastern border as a protection against German invasion and that the Germans retaliated by erecting their own system of fortifications along their western border, which we knew as the Siegfried Line, but which the Germans called the Westwall.

Events now were moving fast. Our XX Corps reported mass enemy movements toward Luxembourg and Germany. At the German border attempts were made by the Gestapo to halt and turn back some of the retreating German units and rioting resulted at several points.

In the south, General Patch's Seventh American Army had advanced to within seven miles of Lyon, was closing up to our southern flank and was soon to make liaison with us. All this time the Germans were seeking revenge by bombing London with robots and on 2 September the first of these was sent over Paris.

A French civilian, just returned from inside Germany, reported to our G-2, Intelligence, that the Germans were arming civilians, even boys, and that girls were being used to man the antiaircraft guns. Also, the retreating Germans for the first time deliberately destroyed a French town before leaving, when they sacked and burned Martincourt.

But the Germans were still fighting desperately. In the XII Corps' area the corps' main telephone wires were cut three times during the night of 3-4 September. We were warned that the closer we got to Germany the more likely were incidents like that to happen and the greater danger there would be from sniping.

Destruction of enemy materiel reached such a rate by 5 September that orders were issued from higher headquarters that no more locomotives or railroad cars should be destroyed, as we wanted to capture and use them ourselves. On that 5 September our air forces destroyed 29 field guns, 985 motor cars, 777 horse-drawn vehicles, 42 locomotives and 108 railroad cars, all behind German lines. No wonder their transportation was in chaos!

At noon of that day the Third Army finally lost control of its great VIII Corps in far away Brittany. It passed to the Ninth U. S. Army, which had now become operational under Lt. General William Simpson. And it was on that day that Bulgaria asked for an armistice.

At this time we captured intact and operational the first German night fighter planes. The Third Army had captured two large air fields north of Chalons and northwest of Rheims. The one near Rheims had concrete runways and we lost no time in making them operational for our own air. The Krauts had decamped so fast that they burned some of their own planes on the ground and left the night fighters unharmed, filled with gas, with their full radar equipment and with their guns loaded. All they needed was a pilot at the controls to take the air. Why they had not been flown away to safety by the enemy is a mystery.

On 6 September patrols of the Third Army entered Germany and penetrated the Siegfried Line in two places.

On the same day Third Army patrols entered the city of Metz and found practically no enemy troops there.

Thousands of gallons of gasoline were being delivered to our forward units by the Air Forces, but newspaper correspondents at Supreme Allied Headquarters were told that further advances were delayed by the difficulty of bringing up supplies.

We were getting short of gasoline and other critical items, due to the extreme length of our own supply lines and the needs of other armies. Priority on all supplies was taken from the Third Army and given to the First U. S. Army and the British to the north to enable them to come up on a line with the Third.

The lull occasioned by the fuel shortage was all to the Kraut's advantage. He rushed reinforcements and supplies, not only into Metz but also into the Siegfried Line, and many weary, bloody weeks were to pass before they would be taken.

We of the Third Army were reluctant to see this happen. In the campaign of a few short weeks, General Patton and his Third Army had captured the imagination of the world. The dash had been made, not against the antiquated, poorly equipped armies of Poland, France or Belgium, where Hitler had achieved his blitzkrieg triumphs, but against the cream of the vaunted Wehrmacht, thoroughly trained and seasoned after four years of actual fighting.

Our boys had met the toughest and cruelest of the German troops and had beaten them. General Patton had outguessed and outmaneuvered the cleverest of their generals and tied them in tactical knots time and again.

He had driven through the enemy lines at breakneck speed, had smashed them at every stand through Normandy, Brittany, along the Loire and north and south of Paris. Every river across France to the German border, streams that should have been defense lines for a properly retiring army but were useless to a defeated army, had been bridged by our victorious troops, and now our men had been inside the fortress city of Metz, one of the strongest in Europe, had been into and through the Maginot Line and over the German border and into the boasted Siegfried Line.

The morale of our troops was at its highest. They had

gone forward more than 400 miles in a little over 30 days. They had tasted victory and were riding the crest of the wave. The feeling of all was that Germany was reeling and "hanging on the ropes." If we could possibly have been reinforced in early September, even with only three or four divisions, and could have been given continued priority on supplies, we felt that our intrepid troops could have dashed completely through the Siegfried Line, cut north through Germany and come up in the rear of the German divisions in the Pas de Calais, even as had been done with the Seventh German Army in Normandy. Is it much wonder that we were deeply disappointed?

We also felt, and felt strongly, that we could have dealt piecemeal with the enemy divisions being brought down from Denmark and Holland, for once the Siegfried Line was penetrated and turned before the enemy could rally his demoralized forces to man its defenses, there was no other prepared defense line which he could have held.

This was the way we looked at the situation in those early days of September.

In its lightning campaign, the Third Army had liberated 41,000 square miles of enemy-held territory and had captured 94,200 prisoners of war, besides inflicting on the enemy an estimated loss of 85,700 wounded and 29,900 killed. In the territory taken were these important cities, the population figures being pre-war.

Nantes, 178,736; Nancy, 112,366; Rheims, 109,081; Angers, 78,693; Rennes, 87,112; LeMans, 74,380; Orleans, 63,638, and Troyes, 56,750.

The great Battle of France was practically at an end, or drawing to its close, and the Third Army was brought virtually to a standstill, knowing that before it lay the enemy's strongest defense works, virtually unmanned and within its grasp.

Even the German radio apparently expected quick penetration and seizure of the Siegfried defenses, for it began preparing German public opinion for the shock by telling them the fortifications were outmoded and without enough depth for modern warfare. Yet, when we later attacked them, those same fortifications had been fully manned and equipped and proved a rather tough nut to crack.

But because we were not to advance farther east for the time being, we did not have an easy and a restful time. Not even in the areas safely behind our mobile ground forces was there any quiet. The Germans kept up persistent, desperate efforts to cut our supply lines. They made bomb raid after bomb raid on the bridges at Verdun, Chalons and Nancy.

On 7 September our XX Corps cavalry crossed the Moselle River. We had a tragic experience, however, with two groups of the 80th Infantry Division, which also crossed the river, at Pont-a-Mousson. Both of these groups ran into heavy resistance and simply disappeared. They were killed or captured; at all events, nothing was heard from them again.

The Germans had prepared for a determined stand along the Moselle for a stretch of 30 miles between Metz and Nancy, and they reacted strongly to every probing we gave them.

But by now they were scraping the bottom of the manpower barrel. A new division was identified on the XII Corps front which had been activated only on 2 August, little more than a month before. A prisoner captured from this division at Nancy said that it was made up of men returning from hospital and men picked up on leave in various sections of Germany. Elements of several new armored divisions also were appearing on our front.

For the third time in this war, the German border now was crossed again. On 12 September the British Broadcasting Corporation announced: "The invasion of Germany has begun!" The 28th Division of the First U. S.

Army, it reported, had crossed the border from the Grand Duchy of Luxembourg and already was five miles inside Germany, in strength. The other two times that enemy troops had been on German soil in World War II were in 1939, when a French patrol penetrated a short distance, and the crossing by our own Third Army patrols six days before this announcement.

The same day came word that the Third and Seventh Armies finally had made contact south of Troyes, when their patrols met. General Patch's Seventh, landing on the Mediterranean coast of France, had made a great sweep up from the south to join us.

We learned on 16 September, from a captured German document, that von Rundstedt was back in command of the German armies in the west. He was one German general whose capabilities were highly regarded on our side, an old Wehrmacht commander who had been entrusted by Hitler with direction of the trials which purged the generals accused in connection with the bombing attempt on Hitler's life the preceding 20 July.

Our headquarters got quite a chuckle out of a sardonic prisoner captured by troops of the XX Corps. He apparently was fed up with the war, with Hitler and with Nazism in general. With cool cynicism he told his American questioners a joke which he said was making the rounds in the German army, to the effect that Hitler's secret weapon that he had been promising for so long and which was now said to be about ready, actually was an all-rubber submarine which was to "encircle the British Isles continually until they are erased."

All the best efforts the Germans could muster to hold the Moselle front solidly came to nothing. Nancy had fallen to the XII Corps and units already were 25 to 30 miles east of the river.

On the 20th there was a heavy counter-attack against

the 4th Armored Division near Arracourt by elements of at least two enemy divisions, other troops and about 150 tanks. The battle lasted through a day and a night and 53 enemy tanks were knocked out.

World news kept filtering in to us. We learned, through liaison channels and from the radio, that: The British were pushing on into Holland; the Canadians were closing in on Dunkerque; coastal towns in England still were taking big shells from across the Channel; flying bombs still were being sent over England and causing heavy damage; the Russians had started a new drive along the Vistula with 40 divisions; the Germans had evacuated Crete and the Aegean islands; in the Pacific, American troops which had landed on Halmahera already had airfields in operation; President Roosevelt and Prime Minister Churchill had finished their talks in Quebec; the siege of Brest was reported in its final stages, with the Germans starting to fire the houses; the blackout in Britain had become a dimout when street lamps were turned on for the first time in five years, and so on. In the midst of all our activities this was interesting news from all over the world.

In mid-September the opposing fronts in the west appeared as follows:

Opposite the British Second and the First U. S. Army in the north was the First German Paratroop Army.

Opposite the Third U. S. Army (XX Corps) were remnants of the German Seventh Army, which had been largely destroyed in Normandy. Opposite our XII and XV Corps was the German First Army.

Opposite the Seventh U. S. Army in the south was the German Nineteenth Army.

Now the XX Corps, attacking Metz, found out just what we had feared would happen—that it was being reinforced strongly. They reported it was defended principally by SS troops, the Nazi fanatics, and prisoners said Himmler in person was directing them. With that sort of set-up we could be sure we faced a terrific fight.

One day our airmen reported they had come in contact with several new enemy planes, rocket-propelled, which they said were of an entirely new type. They described the planes as merely a flying wing, and said the only ones they had been able to hit were some coming head-on at our planes. They were so fast that it was impossible to hit them as they passed to one side. The wing span was given as about 27 feet and it was reported they needed no special landing fields, as they could skid in on almost any sort of field.

They were believed to climb, at sea level, at a rate of 5,000 feet per minute and above that at about 10,000 feet per minute. Their horizontal speed was estimated at 525 to 600 miles an hour, and they carried two 40-mm or two 30-mm cannons.

War activities north and south of us drew our attention, not only as subjects of keen general interest but because they directly affected our own situation and our future.

On the north, the great Allied Airborne drop in the Rhine delta near Arnheim and Nijmegen was carried out, the largest use of airborne troops yet attempted. There was general military agreement that if it was successful in seizing the Nijmegen crossing of the Rhine, its prime purpose, the war would be vastly shortened, since the crossing would have been beyond the Siegfried defenses and would have laid the whole vast north German plain open and defenseless.

Unfortunately, it did not succeed. The armored troops were unable to make contact with the Airborne forces east of the river and suffered heavy losses.

The event south of us was of a more cheering nature.

It was the surrender on 21 September of General Elster and 19,536 German prisoners, including 744 officers. General Elster haughtily told an interpreter that he wanted to surrender to the Third U. S. Army, but actually he and his men were taken south of the Loire River by the 83d Division, now serving with the Ninth U. S. Army, which had come up on the line.

Taken from the surrendered prisoners was a total of 34,000,000 French francs. It may safely be left to the reader's imagination where and how they had come in possession of this wealth. In addition to the soldier prisoners, there were 2,000 animals, 300 motor vehicles and 2,000 horsedrawn vehicles. In the long columns were a number of German marines and also air force personnel, some of them pilots, serving as infantry.

Finally, on 25 September, higher headquarters put a restraining order on the Third Army, prohibiting any further advances until the order was lifted.

10

Line of the Moselle

(25 Sept.-7 Nov. 1944)

IN order that the lay reader may understand more fully
how our modern American armies could make the
extended drives they did in France, how the men could
subsist at the front, how P.W.'s were handled, etc., it
might be interesting here to explain a few things that
otherwise might not be clear.

Practically all of General Patton's orders at the front
were given orally, as were those of his commanders. This,
of course, speeded things up. Sometimes an oral order
would be followed with a written one—just for the record
—but not always. Frequently operational directives were
given in writing, but that was usually all.

General Patton always had more infantry divisions in
his army than he had armored divisions. In all of his
thrusts, he accompanied or at least closely followed his
armored spearheads with infantry units, mounted in trucks.
The trucks for this job were drawn from the army pool
of Quartermaster Truck Battalions. Sometimes whole
infantry divisions were shuttled forward the same way.

In feeding a fast-moving army, the emphasis is placed
on nourishment and portability. Palatability may suffer,
but then no army would be an army if it didn't gripe
about the food. There were 5 kinds of Army rations:

94

A—which was practically all fresh or frozen food, served in camp or permanent quarters; fresh meat, vegetables, fruit, butter, bread, etc. B—or (10 in 1—enough food for 3 meals for 10 men for 1 day)—powdered eggs and powdered milk, cereal, coffee, canned butter, canned roast beef and other meats, canned fruit, dried vegetables, crackers, jam, etc. Two hot meals could be served out of this ration which was all packed in 1 box or carton C—small cans of mixtures of meat and vegetables, beans, jam, crackers, powdered drink, sugar, cereal, etc. D—an emergency ration of solid rich chocolate. K—done up in a neat, waterproof cardboard package about the thickness of an average book but narrower. The outside was camouflaged so that if left on the ground it would not show from the air. Each package contained one meal for 1 man and was marked Breakfast, Dinner or Supper. Breakfast contained fruit bar, nescafé, sugar, crackers and a small can of cooked ham and eggs. Dinner and supper contained a can of cheese or potted meat, crackers, orange or lemon powder, sugar, chocolate or other candy, cigarettes and chewing gum.

Both C and K rations could be eaten cold, or heated if preferred, and each man carried one or two meals on his person, and all vehicles had rations aboard. Many men carried parafin pocket heaters or candles and emergency small gasoline stoves were issued for outposts, wire crews and other small groups.

All units had large two-burner gasoline ranges and wherever possible kitchens were set up where hot meals could be cooked, and the men either rotated back to them or hot food was sent up in insulated cans.

Frequently in the preparation of hot meals, a mixture of the various rations was used. All the rations, particularly K were said to be well balanced and rich in vitamins.

P.W.'s (prisoners of war) are a great drag on the

mobility of an army. They must be guarded, fed and moved. After capture, they were taken back usually on foot to the regimental, division and corps cages under guard, for interrogation. These cages were hastily constructed barbed-wire structures, captured German enclosures or old barracks or other buildings. One of the Geneva Convention international rules of war is that P.W.'s shall have quarters and rations equal to those of the capturing troops.

After interrogation at the corps cage, the P.W.'s were then, within 24 hours, sent back in returning Q.M. ration trucks, usually with one guard per truck in which about 40 P.W.'s were transported, to the Army P.W. enclosure. Here they were again interrogated and kept from 48 hours to a week, when they were shipped back by truck or train to the Communication Zone in the rear areas.

By 25 September our days of wide open warfare and of spectacular advances were over for the time.

Now with the first onset of bad weather, we were forced into a kind of combat we had not experienced before. It amounted almost to positional combat and for a fast-swinging, hard-punching outfit such as General Patton's it was not easy.

Even though halted by higher authority General Patton and his army never went on the defensive. The General did not believe in defense, except in the rarest instances and then only while preparing to attack. Even during this period of apparent defense, he never let the enemy rest, but kept him anxious and worried and off balance.

I doubt very much that the Germans ever even suspected that he had orders to remain on a restraining line. I have no doubt they thought that they, themselves, had finally stopped him.

And so now we came to the toughest and meanest job we had tackled so far, possibly the nastiest we had.

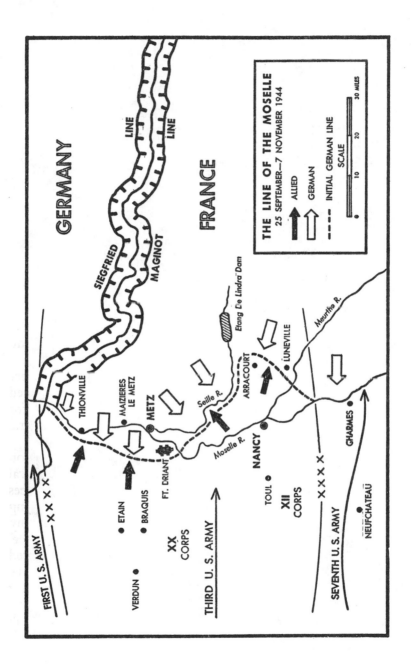

THE LINE OF THE MOSELLE
25 SEPTEMBER—7 NOVEMBER 1944

ALLIED
GERMAN
INITIAL GERMAN LINE
SCALE
0   10   20   30 MILES

GERMANY

FRANCE

SIEGFRIED LINE

MAGINOT LINE

Etang De Lindra Dam

Meurthe R.

THIONVILLE

MAIZIERES
LE METZ

METZ

FT. DRIANT

Seille R.

ARRACOURT

LUNEVILLE

Moselle R.

NANCY

CHARMES

ETAIN

BRAQUIS

VERDUN

TOUL

XII CORPS

NEUFCHATEAU

FIRST U. S. ARMY

XX CORPS

THIRD U. S. ARMY

SEVENTH U. S. ARMY

October and November are usually the rainy season in that region of France, and they lived up to their reputation. There was almost continuous drenching, cold rain, day after day. Pools of water lay everywhere, some of them like good-sized lakes, and the mud was almost unbelievable. It was deep, slimy and slippery. Leather and clothing mildewed and got musty, metal began to rust. Entirely aside from fighting the enemy, there was a constant battle to keep equipment clean and usable and to try to keep oneself as dry as possible. It was a thoroughly miserable time for everybody.

Then the rivers and smaller streams began to overflow from the heavy rains and in places our men sloshed about constantly in deep water.

To top off the misery, the weather turned cold and raw and the men's feet began to freeze. Many of them got "trench feet," the affliction which first came to world attention in the early days of trench warfare in World War I. It is caused by continuous cold and dampness, which slow the circulation of blood to the legs and feet.

General Patton was very solicitous for the comforts of his men. He visited front line units himself and had his liaison officers make daily visits to units to get the low-down on the needs and to report each day on the situation. Orders were flashed to the United States to rush thousands of pairs of galoshes and heavy overshoes, wool socks and long woolen underwear, which were most necessary under the circumstances.

Medical instructions were issued to the troops on how to avoid "trench feet." They were told to change to dry socks at every opportunity and to massage their feet at least once a day to restore the circulation. When the Old Man heard a report of a unit where extra socks were not issued or where there appeared an over-average number of cases of "trench feet," he relieved the unit commander at once.

We stayed in the open, in fields and woods, as we had all across France, until late September, when all Third Army units were ordered, wherever possible, to take whatever cover or shelter could be found in buildings. This applied chiefly, of course, to units in reserve. Men in the front lines always took what shelter they could find, but seldom found any. General Patton kept his troops in the open as long as possible, because he felt the army was much more mobile that way, and offered less vulnerable targets.

In late September, Third Army Headquarters moved out of a woods in the vicinity of Braquis and into the town of Etain, east of Verdun. On 11 October we moved again to the city of Nancy, where XII Corps Headquarters had been for some time.

Then another complication arose. The Moselle River rose another 30 inches, giving us new floods. This was partly due to the fact that our airmen had bombed the Etang de Lindre dam on the Seille River, which flows north roughly parallel to the Moselle and a few miles east of it and empties into the Moselle at Metz. The dam, although fairly shallow, stored millions of tons of water. It posed a constant source of danger should the enemy blow it after part of our troops had advanced beyond. To avoid this and get rid of the danger before starting a major operation, the General ordered the air to bomb it, and they did.

To understand our situation, militarily, in this period, it is necessary to know something of the terrain. The Moselle River runs roughly north about 165 miles east of Paris. It is a stream with many bends and loops.

On the Moselle line where we had come to a halt there are two cities. Nancy is about 50 miles south of Metz, on the west bank of the river. Metz is on the east.

Our troops had crossed the Moselle at several places.

Patton in a typical moment during a tour of inspection and encouragement.

Generals Patton and Bradley, and Field Marshal Montgomery discuss operations.

A Third Army tank destroyer fires on a German-held factory in France. The factory changed hands several times in a few days fighting.

Signal Corps

Third Army troops advancing through French woods to establish a machine-gun position overlooking a Nazi-held town near the Franco-German border.

Patton escorting American labor leaders on an inspection tour of the warfront. With Patton are David J. McDonald, president of the United Steel Workers, and Sherman H. Dalrymple, president of the United Rubber Workers.

Escorted tours of this kind are part of a fighting general's work.

Third Army troops salute the American flag as it is raised on the surrendered fort St. Blaise, Metz. This fort fell 26 November 1944 as the Third Army advanced toward Saarbrucken.

Typical of the young desperados thrown into the fight by the
Germans as they attempted to stem the Allied flood.

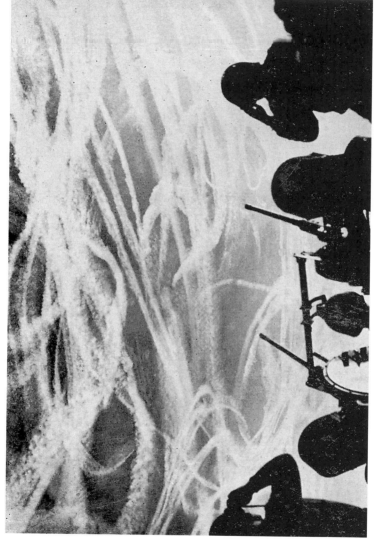

Signal Corps

Visible trails left by invisible Allied and German planes over Bastogne on Christmas Day 1944. The clear weather that allowed Allied planes to operate was the best Christmas present the ground troops could have had during the Battle of the Bulge.

Our XII Corps had a bridgehead on the east bank to a depth of 25 to 30 miles beyond Nancy. Our XX Corps also had forces south and east of Metz, although at the same time the Heinies still had troops on the west of the river in the forts surrounding Metz. During the following weeks the Heinies feverishly brought up reserves to Metz itself and to the 20-odd forts surrounding it.

These forts were among the most formidable in the world and were all underground, in the high hills surrounding the city as will be explained in more detail in the following chapter.

In addition to SS troops, and other reinforcements, the Germans also brought up hundreds of Todt workers who labored continually building new earthworks and other fortifications around the city itself, as well as improving and extending the forts surrounding the city.

During this period our bridgeheads across the Moselle River were strengthened and reinforced. Third Army, for the most part, patrolled and held the enemy on its front by aggressive thrusts here and there. It also made limited objective attacks to seize high ground or critical terrain features.

At this time our XX Corps with the 7th Armored Division and the 5th Infantry Division was making slow progress against the outer forts of Metz. The 90th Division of the same corps was still along the Moselle River to the north and was meeting a serious enemy threat from the north and east. General Patton immediately ordered a task force organized to assist in meeting this threat. It was named Task Force Polk, after its commander, who was Colonel Polk, the C.O. of the 3d Cavalry. This task force was composed of part of HQ. 3d Cavalry, a tank company, a reconnaissance troop of the 43d Cavalry, a group from the 90th Infantry Division, some engineers and also some French Forces of the Interior (F.F.I.). Task Force Polk attacked the German force threatening the north flank of the 90th Division and disorganized them, and then acted as a reconnaissance screen on the north.

The whole front of the XX and the XII Corps was ablaze continually with artillery fire and attacks and counter-attacks.

XX Corps reported extremely heavy enemy artillery fire during these days, but they also reported an increasing number of "duds" among the enemy shells—between 30 and 40 per cent. This latter point was encouraging to old timers from the last war. How well we remembered during the fighting from the Marne to the Vesle River and on towards the Aisne, during July and August, 1918, how every Boche shell was good, and always exploded. Later on in the Argonne in late September and October we figured that 20 to 30 per cent of their shells were duds, and in late October between 40 and 60 per cent failed to explode—and then the Armistice of 11 November came. Could it be that, as in the first World War, German materials and workmanship were getting poorer, and that this was a sign that the end of the war was drawing near? We hoped so. At the front, one's sensibilities are alert to even the smallest points which may be significant.

Due to the more stable conditions of the front our artillery contribution to our attack had been increasing. The enemy artillery fire had also been increasing, and their fire was particularly active and troublesome in the areas of our bridgeheads across the Moselle and Meurthe Rivers. In general, we had, at this time, a preponderance of about three or four to one in artillery along the whole front. Our daily expenditure of artillery ammunition was 700 tons per day.

On 27 September our air forces dropped 21 tanks of incendiary Napalm on Ft. Driant four miles south of Metz. General Hobart R. Gay, then our Deputy Chief, later Chief of Staff, witnessed this experiment with General

Patton from a hillside. He gave us a very vivid description at Staff conference next morning. The 21 planes came over and dived on the very top of the fort. Flames shot up much higher than a house from the first hit. There was a great explosion and smoke went up into the air about 4,000 feet, and debris went in every direction. One of our reconnaissance planes kept flying around and directing the bombers and also giving an eye-witness account of the thing, by radio, from the air. When the German anti-aircraft guns on the ground opened up on our planes, and the flack got fairly heavy, our artillery concealed in the nearby hills effectively silenced them. This was another example of the close cooperation of our air and ground forces. In this whole operation we lost no planes.

During these days our air was skip-bombing the Krauts, preventing them from bringing up supplies and reinforcements. The planes would swoop low and skip bombs into railroad tunnels. The bombs would go in several hundred yards and explode inside the tunnel, thus closing it up, and making it difficult to repair the damage. One day two of our bombers saw a German train about to enter a long tunnel. One plane came up from behind and the other flew round to the other end of the tunnel. After the train was inside they both skipped their bombs into opposite ends of the tunnel and sealed the Kraut train inside.

On 28 September, after Ft. Driant had been attacked from the air, as mentioned, the 5th Infantry Division (XX Corps) attacked the fort and advanced as far as the moat surrounding the inner fort.

On this date the XV Corps which had been operating in the south reverted to the Seventh U. S. Army and a slight change was made in Army boundaries giving the towns of Charmes and Luneville to the Seventh Army.

At the same time the 7th Armored Division of the XX Corps was assigned to the First Army and moved north into its zone. Another infantry division, however, the 83d, had arrived and was attached to XX Corps. While this division was arriving the 90th Infantry Division repulsed a strong enemy counter-attack. Many enemy casualties were reported, and a very interesting fact also reported was that the prisoners of war taken were all extremely drunk.

At this time more jet-propelled planes were seen over Germany by our air forces. Also a rocket going straight up into the air at an estimated speed of 3,000 miles per hour was reported. 29 September was one of the biggest days for our air forces. The XIX Tactical flew 39 missions, 573 sorties, dropped 231 tons of bombs and 36 Napalm bombs. Twelve enemy planes were destroyed on the ground and four in the air. We lost seven planes. In all sixty enemy aircraft were seen in the air.

The Claims of the XIX Tactical on this day were 1 bridge, 58 locomotives, 127 railroad cars, 2 armored cars, 35 motor vehicles, 18 field guns, 6 planes on the ground—all destroyed. In addition 2 airfields were attacked, 72 railroad cuts made, 6 ammunition dumps hit, 2 railroad tunnels closed and 1 railroad bridge hit. Very heavy German flack was encountered.

The Metz forts in our front were proving tough opposition. The air attacks which we had been making on these underground forts were using a great many of our fighter bombers without much profit. A 1,000 pound bomb was seen to bounce off the steel and concrete top of Ft. Driant and explode in another place. Our air force concluded that we were wasting our fighter-bomber effort.

The fighting on the Third Army front became increasingly slow and difficult amid the mud and rain and cold.

On the XX Corps front 6 P.W.'s were taken behind our lines from the 48th German Division. They were in civilian clothes and stated that they had been sent in as spies.

On the XII Corps front a night counterattack against the 4th Armored Division was not repulsed till daylight.

In the XII Corps zone also our air bombed a woods and flushed out some tanks which our armor knocked off as they emerged from the woods.

In early October a number of German P.W.'s were taken wearing American field jackets and helmets. These clothes had, of course, been taken from our prisoners or from our American dead.

Each day heavy fire continued coming from Ft. Driant and the other Metz forts.

On 2 October it was reported that the 12th SS and the 2d Panzer Grenadier Divisions had been withdrawn from the front, probably for refittting. (Note—these later appeared in the Battle of the Bulge).

By 4 October our XX Corps' 5th Infantry Division had two companies of infantry and two tank platoons inside Ft. Driant. About one-third of the fort was in our hands. The fort itself was actually over a mile in length and about a half mile wide.

Our G-2 estimated that the enemy fighter plane strength in our front at this time was about 800 planes. It was therefore believed that the enemy could make a strong concentrated attack at any one point.

The 5th Infantry Division reported that for the second time, the enemy had fired propaganda leaflets by artillery. It was a clumsy propaganda, the chief theme being that even though they had been promised it, our troops were not getting home by Christmas.

During all of this bitter fighting our Third Army Psychological Warfare had been continually propagandizing the enemy. Newspapers in German were dropped three times a week over the enemy lines, giving them the news. Frequent direct radio broadcasts were made in German. Since 1 August, 1,500,000 leaflets had been fired into enemy lines by our artillery; 5,000,000 leaflets had been dropped by fighter bombers and 40,000,000 leaflets had been dropped on towns and cities by heavy bombers. Over the radio, letters from home taken from P.W.'s were read to the troops; the hopelessness of their situation and cause was emphasized. They were told that the Nazis were sacrificing their lives playing for time for themselves. Instructions were given on how to surrender to the Americans.

General Patton continued to visit front line units every day to find out exactly what the situations were and to encourage the men and their commanders.

One bleak, cold, rainy day I suggested to a very good friend of mine in the headquarters, Col. William E. Griffin, that we visit the prisoner of war enclosure at Toul, and interview some of the prisoners first hand, to see if we could figure out what they were thinking and see how the German mind worked. When we reached the big P.W. caserne or barracks, we asked the Provost Marshal to give us an interpreter, as neither of us spoke German.

They brought the prisoners to us at random, but all three of them happened to be from the 11th Panzer Division which was in the front of our XII Corps and was one of Hitler's tough outfits. The three interviewed were all from the armored infantry of that division.

The first man they brought in to us was a tall youth, 23 years old, he said. He had light hair and blue eyes and looked like a farm boy. He was an extremely stupid individual and didn't know what it was all about. He reminded us of a dumb ox, so we sent him back to the pen.

The next P.W. was a rather short, slight man of 38, with black hair and sunken eyes. He told us he had been a truck driver and when we showed surprise that he was captured with the 11th Panzer Division he told us the following story. It seems he had been driving his truck up toward the front one night when our night fighters (Black Widows) strafed the road along which he was driving and he being very much excited, ran his truck into a tree and smashed it. The Germans were so angry at him for smashing his truck that they beat him and gave him three days in the clink on bread and water.

When they released him, as further punishment they put him in a front line unit, the 11th Panzer Division, and as still further punishment, in an outpost of the armored infantry. He related how when the Americans attacked, he stayed down in his foxhole and surrendered to them after they had passed over.

We next asked that a German officer be brought in, so they brought in a first lieutenant who had commanded one of the armored infantry companies. He was short, stocky, husky and very military. His heels clicked as he stepped before us. He said he was 27 years old and was one of the toughest, meanest and hardest individuals I have ever seen in my life. I would have hated to have been under his power. He was haughty and proud and cocky. He also had a scar on the side of his face either from a wound or a saber mark.

We started to question him and he was so cynical and sarcastic that we showed him no consideration for we were anxious to see how he reacted. One of our questions was "Lieutenant, do you think that the Germans are really supermen—a superior race?"

His eyes flashed, and his heels clicked and he stiffened up and said:

"Of course they are a superior race. There is no doubt about it!"

"Well," we said, "if you are such a superior race, why have you allowed the low grade Americans and British to chase you all the way across France from the beaches to here, a distance of some 400 miles?"

He looked us in the eye, and snapped back, "That is only the fortunes of war. We have been retreating lately, but you have retreated before, and you will again. You will see. In the end we will win."

Our next question was, "Where is Herr Hitler?" (He had not been heard of or made any speeches lately).

His answer to that was, "I do not know. Herr Hitler is a politician. Possibly he is in Moscow, with Stalin," he added with a grin. (This, of course, was to throw doubt in our minds about our Russian allies, suggesting that possibly Hitler and Stalin were cooking up a separate peace or an agreement of some kind).

We then asked him why Germany did not act intelligently and realize she was licked and try to make the best peace terms she could before her country was invaded as it was surely going to be. We told him that there were now seven Allied armies facing Germany in the West alone, not counting the Russians in the east—4 American Armies, 1 British, 1 Canadian and 1 French; and that German forces were outnumbered at least two to one.

To these statements and questions he answered, "That is all propaganda—your propaganda. You would not expect me to believe it, would you? For, of course, it is not true."

The Heinies, I fear, were a misguided, misinformed and a rather stupid people, for what we were telling him was true.

Our last question of interest was, "Lieutenant, if you are the superman that you say you are, why did you surrender? Why did you give up to the miserable Americans? Why didn't you fight to the finish and then possibly in the end you would have been victorious?"

His eyes really flashed now, a scowl came over his face and he stiffened up, as he replied, "I did fight. My armored company was down to only sixteen left. The Americans outnumbered us and had surrounded us. There was no use fighting any more." And he added sarcastically, "What do you think I am, a damn Jap?"

As October moved along our air reported that the enemy flack was getting stronger every day. Enemy defensive preparations were getting stronger also, they were digging in, bringing up reinforcements, manning the old Maginot forts in our front, and there was heavy traffic both east to west and west to east—horse-drawn and motor, behind the German lines.

There was heavy enemy resistance along our whole front, and our artillery fire against the Metz forts was having little effect.

One of the two sound trucks which the Germans had been using up in the front line to broadcast propaganda, in which they named the Commanding General of the 5th Division and some of the other officers, was destroyed by our artillery fire, much to the delight of our doughboys.

The enemy was beginning to use dogs in places to assist their outpost guards. Their patrols penetrating behind our lines at night frequently strung wires across the roads at the height to decapitate our men speeding along in open jeeps. To prevent this all our jeeps then had steel T-rods welded on the fronts to cut this wire.

A civilian who came through the lines reported a new division from the Russian front was due to arrive on our First Army front in the near future. A P.W. named still another division from the same front about to arrive on our front.

Many of the P. W.'s captured at this time were disgusted and disillusioned. One of them being interrogated said that Hitler had made only one true statement in his life. That was when he was first coming into power, when he said, "Let me have Germany for ten years, and at the end of that time you will not be able to recognize it!" Later when we ourselves saw the actual destruction and devastation in the German cities wrought by our air force and our artillery we got the full significance of this cynical statement.

P.W.'s reported that commanding officers had been ordered to shoot every tenth man if their unit retreated.

During these early days of October our XX Corps (5th Infantry Division and Task Force Warnock) was continuing the attack against Ft. Driant. Two groups were working inside this enormous fort. One group was working underground, through the tunnels and passages clearing out the debris, breaking through iron doors from one compartment to another. The other group was working above ground, trying to batter doors in, and keep enemy guns from firing. The group above ground gained about 250 yards, but was forced back and had to give up all but 50 yards. Two things caused a great deal of trouble and many casualties. Disappearing pillboxes, which, invisible until they had been passed, would come up out of the ground and open fire from the rear. The other was very accurately adjusted artillery fire. It came from the outside of the fort but was apparently adjusted from inside as it followed closely even very small groups and individuals as they moved around the fort.

Finally on 13 October the elements of the 5th Infantry Division and Task Force Warnock were ordered to withdraw from Ft. Driant under cover of darkness. General Patton had other plans.

On this same date a new division, the 95th Infantry, arrived and was assigned to XX Corps to relieve the 5th Infantry Division which had taken a considerable beating in its underground and overground attack against the citadel of Ft. Driant.

The 90th Division of XX Corps was all during this time engaged in some of the bitterest fighting of the war, north of Metz, especially around the town of Maizieres Les Metz. This town changed hands several times in house to house fighting and for a couple of weeks part of the town was held by the Heinies and part by our 90th Division boys. One little incident showed how close to each other the opposing forces were. An American soldier went into a kitchen of one of the houses which had just been captured, in order to warm his K ration on the stove. As he pushed open the door into the kitchen, he surprised six Germans gathered around the stove preparing themselves a meal. Thinking there were other Americans with the one, they all threw up their hands and surrendered. So he captured them and also the meal which had just been cooked.

So bitter was the fighting about this town of Maizieres Les Metz and so great the number of German mines and booby traps, that two months later bodies of dead Heinies were still lying among the wreckage, partly covered with snow. Our men did not want to risk losing a leg or being blown to bits by a mine or booby trap just to remove a German body.

From the seige of Aachen up north in the First Army area, came an amusing story. The 1106th Combat Engineer Battalion, in an attempt to discredit and make fun of Hitler's promise and threat of new secret weapons, found a street car in the outskirts of Aachen. They loaded it up with explosives and skidded it down a hill into the town. It was labelled in large German letters "V-12—

SECRET WEAPON." It exploded in the town.

Despite making fun of Hitler and his secret weapons, however, there were still indications, which we were watching carefully, that the Germans were preparing new weapons. More jet propelled planes were observed almost daily practicing over Germany, and on 15 October several large rockets were observed in the Third Army front going from north to south. They were at a very high altitude, traveling extremely fast and making considerable noise—more than the buzz bombs over London.

Many trains were going in and out of Metz. A column of 75 to 100 vehicles was seen moving from east to west into the city. About half of these vehicles had a Red Cross painted on them.

A 5-man enemy patrol penetrated deep into our lines and attacked and killed a sentry of a Field Artillery Battalion.

The Heinies now began using a loud speaker in the front lines urging our men, in English, to surrender stating that they as P.W.'s, would receive excellent food and treatment. They used almost the same words that we had used to them.

On 16 October the Berlin radio reported that Field Marshal Rommel had died from head injuries due to an automobile accident. The Allied radio, however, stated that the Marshal, the "Desert Fox," had possibly died of head injuries, but that they were due to wounds received from an air bombing in Normandy.

On 18 October a large dump of German military maps found in Brussels by the British showed that as late as 1943 the Germans were still planning to invade Britain.

Some P.W.'s captured from a knocked out tank in 26th Infantry Division zone (XII Corps) were very anxious to know what had happened to our 4th Armored Division. It so happened that it had been withdrawn into reserve for awhile for refitting. These P.W.'s stated that they had a great deal of respect for this division and had nick-named it "Roosevelt's Butchers."

All during these days of bitter fighting and foul weather our American Red Cross continued to do a wonderful job, not only behind the lines for those soldiers pulled out for a few days rest, but practically into the front lines. Every day the Red Cross mobile canteens brought the men hot coffee, doughnuts and cigarettes, and a word or two of cheer from the girls who drove and ran the canteens.

A word too should be said for the U.S.O. shows and the movie stars who visited front line units and entertained the men directly behind the lines. For months all during the worst weather, they continued to appear and give shows in cellars or barns to groups brought back a few hundred yards, in small numbers at a time, from each unit. At one place Marlene Dietrich and a group with her were giving a show in an old barn. Ten minutes after she and they had left the barn, it was entirely demolished by a direct hit from a large German shell.

At this time the Heinies were beginning to scrape the bottom of the manpower barrel, but they were still fighting tenaciously. There were now the equivalent of 4 enemy divisions in the Third Army front and about 50 tanks. This was a decrease of about 150 tanks and 3 infantry divisions since 1 October. It was believed, how-ever, by our G-2 that 5 additional divisions could be brought against us immediately as reinforcements.

On 19 October over the radio, Hitler in a speech an-nounced "Due to failure of some of our allies, the enemy is now on our borders. The purpose of our enemy is to exterminate the German people. A new Peoples Army will be formed in Germany, of men between 16 and 60. Himmler will be in command of this army. Every kilometer will cost our enemy streams of blood. Every German farm will be defended, if not by men, then by women and girls."

We began to encounter a new type of enemy troops. They were called Fortress Battalions and were used in the forts surrounding Metz and in the Maginot and Siegfried Lines. They were for the most part men well past middle age, veterans of World War I, or were boys 15 and 16 years old. Many of the older men had lost a leg or an arm and sometimes an eye, but they could organize the youngsters and could fire a machine gun or rifle from an embrazure in a fort or pillbox.

The Germans were continually improving their defensive positions and doing active patrolling. There were also numerous enemy movements observed in their rear areas.

In a lighter vein and to lesson the tension of the news of the serious, bitter fighting, our Public Relations Officer, Major P. D. Weidmer, who read the briefing notes of the news picked out of the air, at the 0900 Staff meetings, one day stated, "From America it is announed that Gypsie Rose Lee, the famous strip-tease artist, is in Reno to divorce her third husband, to write her second book, and to have her first child." General Patton and the staff always got a big kick out of these quips.

It was now decided to have our heavy bombers attack Ft. Driant with a new type of bomb which was expected to penetrate about 50 feet. The attack was put on, but Ft. Driant still held out.

Mines were being laid by the thousands around Metz and the forts surrounding the city.

The Moselle River had risen 2½ feet since October 15th.

Our artillery fire was being curtailed due to a shortage of ammunition. We, however, supplemented our own artillery by firing captured enemy guns and ammunition.

Several interesting statements and observations were made in our G-2 briefings during these weeks, especially in view of the great German attack in the north in the First Army area, in the Ardennes, a couple of months later.

On 24 October our G-2 reported, "In the 79th Division area, an officer P.W. stated that the 15th Panzer Grenadier Division was being withdrawn from the front, for refitting and reorganizing."

On 27 October, also from our G-2, "The Germans confirm that Von Rundstedt is again commanding in the west, and Guderian is in charge of the eastern front." Also "it appears that the Germans are trying to form a Panzer Army from remnants of Panzer Divisions withdrawn from this front. It is believed they have five such divisions back in Germany now, reorganizing them into this Panzer Army. The G-2, 12th Army Groups, believes that if given enough time, until 1 December, for instance, the Germans might be able to organize a sufficiently strong mobile force to stalemate this western front for the winter."

On 28 October, G-2, "Higher headquarters reports three divisions of the enemy moving from Norway—probable destination Denmark."

29 October, G-2, "At present time there are only three Panzer Divisions on Western front—9th Panzer Division on British front and 11th and 21st Panzer Divisions on Seventh Army front. The rest have been withdrawn and are probably being held in mobile reserve."

7 November, G-2, "12th Army Group reports that Sixth Panzer Army is forming opposite the British front. It is, so far, composed of four Panzer Divisions, the 2d SS Division, the 10th SS Division, 12th SS Division, and the 130 Panzer Lehr Division."

And so the great drama of December 1944 was building up—not unnoticed but uncomprehended.

The front continued active and on fire. Enemy movements were observed behind the lines. Enemy patrols infiltrated through our lines in several places and fired on our rear and flanks. At Onville they cut our telephone wires several times during one evening.

A P.W. taken by the 90th Division reported four reasons for low morale among the Germans:

1. Our artillery fire.
2. Poor food.
3. Absence of German air force.
4. Wet weather which made fox holes untenable.

The P.W. stated that more of them would surrender and become prisoners except that they feared reprisals to their families at home. They also feared bad treatment at our hands after being captured, as they had been told. Another thing they feared was stepping on mines as they came through our lines.

Our air reported that the R.A.F. Transport Command had so far flown 40,000 wounded men from the western front to Britain without a single mishap.

Air also reported at this time that in one German town many civilians were observed in the streets waving white flags.

Flying bombs were again seen over First Army front.

XII Corps G-2 reported that another regiment of the 361st Division had been identified. This division had been reorganized in Holland and was composed 50% of 16-18 year old youths and the balance of returned wounded veterans.

Goebels on the 1 November, urged the German people to fight on and wait for new weapons.

All during these weeks, in addition to sporadic enemy air raids over our front, the Germans were continually firing heavy caliber shells into our Corps and Army Headquarters. Many of these shells were fired from 280-mm railroad guns, which were equivalent to about 11-inch naval guns. They were very annoying, to say the least, as they would drop in the area every few minutes from about 0100 till 0400 or 0500 in the morning. Before daybreak these guns were evidently run on their railroad gun carriages into a tunnel for concealment, for our air was never able to locate them. They caused a number of casualties in the headquarters as well as among the civilian population.

On 7 November in a speech on the 27th anniversary of the October Revolution, Joseph Stalin stated that the Allies are already fighting inside Germany on the west and the east. On the west the Allies were engaging 75 divisions while on the east the Russians were engaging 204 divisions. He stated that 120 German divisions had already been destroyed, and that 30 more, at the present time, were being liquidated. He further stated that the Red Flag would soon be flying over Berlin. He also stated that Great Britain, the United States and Russia must stick together after the war as well as during it.

It was now 7 November. Contrasted with the earlier campaign of the dash across France, this campaign had not been nearly as spectacular.

Only 125 square miles of territory had been taken and 8,481 prisoners of war had been captured. But now— 7 November—Third Army was ready to take off again. The restraining order had been lifted.

11

Capture of Metz and Saar Valley
(8 Nov.-18 Dec.)

THE campaign for the capture of Metz and the Saar
Valley, including the penetrations of the Siegfried
Line, in one of its strongest sectors, was one of the bitterest periods of fighting during the war. During this
period Third Army consisted of two Corps—the XX
Corps, composed of the 10th Armored Division and the
5th, 90th and 95th Infantry Divisions; and the XII Corps,
composed of the 4th and 6th Armored Divisions, and
the 26th, 35th and 80th Infantry Divisions.

During the operation the Third Army front was over
a hundred miles long. Several hundred towns and the
fortified city of Metz, with a pre-war population of 71,317,
were captured with the 1,820 square miles of enemy-held
territory. The greatest part of the territory captured was
very heavily fortified and the weather was foul—cold, rain
and mud. To further show the bitterness of the fighting,
in the little more than a month period, 34,489 prisoners
of war were taken by our two corps and an estimated
82,500 casualties inflicted on the enemy—20,900 killed and
61,600 wounded or a grand total of 118,989 enemy put
out of action.

While the XX Corps was capturing Metz and its surrounding forts and reaching the German border in the
north, the XII Corps drove relentlessly forward in the

south and established two strong bridgeheads over the Saar River and through the Siegfried Line at Saarlautern and Dillingen.

The fortified city of Metz, as has been indicated in the previous chapter, was a tough nut to crack. Never in its long history of over 1500 years had it been taken by assault. The Americans in 1918 were about to start operations against it, when the Armistice of 11 November came. It was in this war analagous to Verdun in World War I, which the Germans tried so long and so hard to take, but which they never did. The only difference was, the American Third Army took Metz.

The city itself is situated ideally for defense on the east bank of the Moselle River. Barbed wire and earth fortifications had been built around the city and in addition to the Moselle River itself, on the west, which is a formidable barrier, large tributaries of the Moselle run on both the north and south sides of the city.

But the greatest defense were the hills which surround it on practically all sides. All of these hills had been organized and built into powerful underground forts over the years, with underground passageways deep in the earth, steel and concrete doors which were placed behind high earth embankments so that they not only could not be seen from the ground, preventing direct artillery fire, but they were also almost impossible to bomb effectively from the air, protected as they were by the earth banks.

There were about twenty of these forts in all, each one with its own name—Forts Orny, Verny, Chesny, Hubert, Jussy, etc.—but Fort Driant, south of the city and on the west bank of the Moselle, Fort Jeanne D'Arc opposite it on the east side of the river, and Fort Verdun were the largest and strongest of them all.

There were three types of forts; forts from the Franco-Prussian War of 1870 and before, the French forts constructed at the time of World War I or right afterwards in conjunction with the Maginot Line, and the German forts constructed during this war.

Most of the guns were of French manufacture. The larger forts had 105-mm howitzers, and 150-mm guns. They were all well stocked with French ammunition and other supplies.

Many of the forts had steel and concrete tops buried under thick layers of earth, and steel and concrete gun embrasures as well as the disappearing guns mentioned in the previous chapter. Ditches and moats, barbed wire and gun emplacements had recently been added, as well as many mine fields. All the bridges into the city of Metz had been mined. All types of Fortress Battalions and other troops had been rushed to the city to man its fortifications, and the only escape gap to the east had been completely closed and was guarded by the Gestapo to insure that all the Germans remained to fight to the bitter end.

This was the iron-shelled nut which General Patton had to crack with his XX Corps on the jump-off on 8 November. During October, as has been pointed out in the previous chapter, the XX Corps commander, Major General Walton H. Walker, had been experimenting with Fort Driant. Task Force Warnock and part of the 5th Infantry Division had penetrated into the center of the underground fort and had been over most of the exterior. It had been the toughest kind of fighting and there had been many casualties, but these had not been in vain, for the experience and knowledge gained helped materially in the attack which ended with the capture of this well-nigh impregnable fortress.

The stronghold was reduced by what may be described as two double envelopments—an inner one toward the heart of the city and another one toward the German border to cut off all chance of relief by any possible reinforcements. The 5th and 95th Infantry Divisions, with some separate tank and tank destroyer battalions, infiltrated through and around the various forts while the 90th Infantry Division secured the northern flank and drove forward there, cutting the city off from the north. The 10th Armored Division moved in after the infantry divisions and later drove all the way to the German border on the southern flank of the Corps.

The city itself was completely surrounded by the 5th and 95th Divisions. The highways and railroads entering the city from the east, which had been used so long to bring up reinforcements and supplies, were cut at last, and the Gestapo no longer needed to mount guard to keep the defenders inside.

With the city once surrounded, a strong drive was made from the southeast into its very heart after heavy bombers had dropped tons of bombs on the city's center and the forts.

Almost simultaneously, the 5th Infantry Division got one road open from the southeast while the 95th Infantry Division captured a bridge in the north. Thus our troops got into the city itself from two directions. Some of the smaller forts fell at the same time, but the stronger ones held out for weeks. The last one did not fall until 14 December. Since the unconquered ones could bring observed fire on all the roads entering Metz as well as on the heart of the city, it was a decidedly unhealthy place to be for some time. How the remaining forts finally were reduced one by one will be described later.

While this attack by the XX Corps was going on against Metz, the XII Corps was driving relentlessly forward in the southern sector, against the most stubborn resistance, directly toward and through the Siegfried Line at one of its strongest points. Here, as at Metz, the Germans had had time to reinforce all the area before the Siegfried Line, to build earthworks, lay barbwire and mine fields and to build road blocks.

Here again General Patton was able to outsmart the Heinies and to improvise surprises for them as he had done with the hedgecutters bolted on the front of tanks which drove through the hedgerows in Normandy.

This time, however, conditions were different. The fields, particularly the valleys and lowlands were filled with water lying on top of the ground, making them boggy and deep with mud. Our most powerful tanks, with their inadequate tracks, sank down into the mud, and could scarcely extricate themselves. They became sitting ducks for the German antitank guns placed behind strongly defended road blocks erected across every road.

In order to overcome this, the General again put his Ordnance Battalions feverishly to work as he had in Normandy, only this time instead of making hedgecutters, they made what were called "duck bills". These duck bills were metal half-cups about the size of your hand, welded on the outside of each joint in the tracks of the tank. The edges turned down and they looked something like the upper half of a duck's bill—hence the name. Since they extended about five inches beyond the outer edge of the tracks of the tank, they gave a total of ten inches more of flotation to the tank, which proved to be enough to allow the tank to travel at full speed over all but the marshiest ground.

With this aid our tanks could quit the roads, as they had in the dash across France in the summertime, and the laboriously constructed roadblocks, which the Krauts had built with so much effort, became all but worthless, since we could now go around them.

Road blocks located in terrain where it was impossible to go around them, were circumvented by another surprise. On a number of ordinary medium tanks he had ordnancemen weld pieces of five and six inch armor plate to the fronts as protection for the most vulnerable spots. From a distance the extra armor plate was not visible, and the tank looked like an ordinary one.

The German 88-mm high velocity antitank guns and the Tiger tanks equipped with these same guns, could outshoot our 75-mm and our 90-mm guns. So when the Krauts, from behind a road block, saw one of our tanks coming directly up the road at them, they thought it would be easy to knock it out.

What a surprise the Heinies got when in our attack on 8 November they saw our duck-billed tanks take off across the fields around their road blocks, right through the mud and water.

And what a second surprise they got when they were sure they would stop our tanks at certain road blocks, where it was impossible to get off the road, and an ordinary looking tank would come right up the center of the road at them, blazing away with its guns, and their shells which had been able to knock out our tanks before seemed to bounce right off the front of them now.

The Siegfried Line, pierced by our XII Corps, ran from Cleve near the Holland border, along the Rhine in many places, all the way to the Swiss border. It was started in 1936. It was given the highest priority in 1938 to 1940, when construction is supposed to have ceased, after the fall of France.

It was designed and planned mainly to oppose armored attacks. For this reason it was strongest where the terrain was favorable for armored attacks, or where it protected a particularly important city or section. It was therefore strongest in the front that Third Army approached. It was built as continuous lines, sometimes two, sometimes three deep, made up of small steel and concrete forts or pillboxes which were mutually supporting. In front of the thinner sections of the line were marshes and low lands. Most guns pointed to the flanks rather than to the front and it was designed to channel attacks of an enemy in certain directions where flank fire could be brought on the elements penetrating. The steep banks, and gulches formed by the Rhine and Moselle rivers formed excellent, natural conditions for flanking fire.

The forts or pillboxes in Third Army front were staggered to a depth of more than three miles and there were 40 of them in each 1,000-yard square. In the same area in other sections of the line, there might be only 20 of these same forts or pillboxes. There were also reserve positions up to 20 miles to the rear. In addition to the pillboxes there were also armored boxes covered with armor plate for headquarters, reserves, ammunition, supplies, etc.

The pillboxes and forts were supported mostly by small arms and antitank guns. In addition there were mine fields and antitank obstacles such as concrete dragons' teeth, curved rails and ditches, some of which were 60 feet wide and could be filled with water. All of these fortifications and obstacles were well camouflaged, particularly since underbrush had grown up around them.

In 1940 the communications within the line were reported to be the very latest and most excellent.

The enemy artillery, for the most part, was placed in the open so it could be moved from place to place.

Air photographs indicated that the fortifications and obstacles were somewhat the same type as encountered on the Normandy beaches.

On 7 November the Forward Command Post (CP) of the XII Corps moved from Nancy over to the east side of the Moselle River into the bridgehead held by our troops. From the foremost location held by our troops there were 30 to 40 miles of heavily fortified French territory before the Siegfried Line itself was reached.

At 0500 8 November, long before daylight, a terrific forty-five minute artillery preparation commenced in which all the guns of both corps took part. Prior to the day of the attack, every artillery battalion had been moved under cover of darkness to a new position. The sky was ablaze with the flashes and the ground shook and rumbled. In this forty-five minutes, over 30,000 rounds of ammunition were fired. At 0545 the infantry divisions jumped off on schedule. Even with all the dangers of the attack, it was a relief to be on the move again and out of the same old mud even though it was only forward into new mud.

The initial attack was successful and our infantry pushed forward about three miles. During the day there was excellent air support and for the first time, in addition to ordinary bombs and strafing, our planes dropped Napalm bombs on enemy foxholes and trenches with good results. Many Heinies were burned to a crisp in their trenches as this jelled gasoline dropped on them from the air.

In the first day of our attack three things stood out:

1. The Germans were unable to stage any sizeable counterattack, (showing that they were surprised and stunned).

2. No enemy armor was encountered.

3. Only one new enemy unit was encountered (a new regiment in 80th Division zone).

However, by the second day the enemy was resisting stubbornly and his air forces were very actively strafing our ground troops. Heavy artillery fire was encountered at our river crossings particularly in the vicinity of Metz.

By the 10th of November our forces were driving forward steadily and our armor was going into action. Our 2d Cavalry had reached Moncourt and Bezauge La Petite and the 26th Infantry Division had gained about seven miles and was now in Chateau-Salins, which had been fortified and was bitterly contested. The 4th Armored Division had now reached a point seven miles north and east of Chateau-Salins and one combat command had crossed the Seille River and was seventeen miles north and east of the same town.

By this time, in the XX Corps zone in the north, the 5th

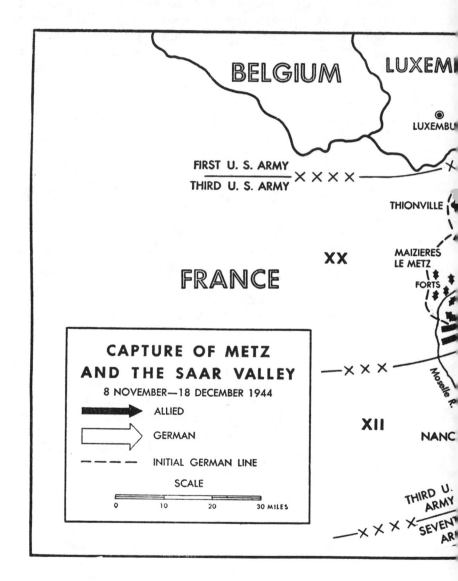

BELGIUM LUXEM

LUXEMBU

FIRST U. S. ARMY
─────────────── × × × × ─── ×
THIRD U. S. ARMY

THIONVILLE

XX

MAIZIERES
LE METZ

FRANCE

FORTS

CAPTURE OF METZ
AND THE SAAR VALLEY
8 NOVEMBER—18 DECEMBER 1944

ALLIED

GERMAN

INITIAL GERMAN LINE

SCALE

0   10   20   30 MILES

── × × × ──

Moselle R.

XII

NANC

THIRD U.
ARMY

── × × × × ── SEVEN
AR

Infantry Division had advanced and had taken its initial objective and the 95th Infantry Division had gained about a mile and a half against the stiffest sort of resistance south of the town of Maizieres les Metz. The 90th Infantry Division had all elements across the Moselle River and had advanced over three miles. One enemy counterattack against them was reported.

On this same day there were the most encouraging reports from our air forces. In addition to our own support by the XIX Tactical Air Force, the Eighth Air Force employed 1476 heavy bombers, escorted by 495 fighters in Third Army front. Over two thousand tons of bombs were dropped on Metz alone. Because of the weather they were forced to bomb through clouds, using pathfinder flare technique. Ten of our heavy bombers and five of the fighters were lost. Fourteen of our XIX Tactical fighters were also lost on this day.

Mr. Churchill disclosed that Britain had been under fire for several weeks from German long range rockets. He said that a number of these missiles, which the Germans called V-2, had landed at widely scattered points. Casualties and damage had so far not been heavy. The rockets weighed about 15 tons and went up into the stratosphere 60 to 70 miles and traveled down at a speed of 3,000 miles per hour—faster than sound. No reliable warning of its approach, therefore, could be given. The range of these rockets was about 250 miles. The rockets made a deeper crater than the flying bomb, but consequently had less blast effect.

By 11 November the close in and the wide envelopment forces of our XX Corps had made progress on both sides of Metz. To the north we had reached a point two and a half miles from the German frontier, and on the south side we had pushed forward up to five miles and had cut the main railroad on the east linking the fortress with the mainland of Germany. A new division was identified—the 272d Volks Grenadier Division.

In the XII Corps zone, the 4th Armored Division and the 35th Infantry Division reported continued stiff resistance in the vicinity of Chateau-Salins, largely by the 11th Panzer Division.

The 26th Infantry Division had identified another new division, the 533d Infantry. This had been formerly on the front of the Seventh Army south of us. The 6th Armored Division took prisoners from an artillery regiment which had just recently moved down from Norway. The Germans were reinforcing against us in an effort to check the Third Army drive.

P.W.'s taken at this time stated that our artillery concentrations on the first day of the attack had been terrifying. Their horses were killed, their guns had to be shuttled and their communications were disrupted. They had been taken completely by surprise, because they figured that the weather was entirely too bad for us to start an attack.

One of my Liaison officers who had paid a visit to a front line division in the XII Corps area on 11 November, told an interesting story when he returned. He said that he was approaching the front out to the east in the vicinity of Chateau-Salins. He was traveling along in his jeep with the top down, and at the moment was passing through a town which had been almost completely destroyed by artillery fire and bombs. Hardly a building remained in the town, only a few walls, and the streets, still littered with rubble, were silent and deserted.

Suddenly he was startled by the ringing of the bells in the tower of the cathedral, which was the only thing standing, the body of the church having been destroyed. He looked at his watch, and saw that it was exactly 11 o'clock and he realized that it was November 11th—Armistice Day. Someone had come back into that town to ring the church bells, as they had rung 26 years before, to celebrate the driving of the Huns from the beloved soil of France. This officer said that with that kind of spirit he felt sure that France would rise again and become once more a really great country.

On 12 November counter-intelligence reported the arrival of two large groups of the enemy with tanks in Third Army front. On this same date the First Army reported that the 116th Panzer Division and the 15th Panzer Grenadier Division had been withdrawn from the line in its front.

The weather continued cold and rainy day after day, imposing added hardships on the troops. All the rivers and streams were swollen and the water was rising. The Moselle River was reported to have reached the highest point in history. Our bridges were frequently washed away by the floods and sometimes the water would rise so high that it would cover our bridges and they would have to be rebuilt. It was almost impossible to get our heavy artillery across. Our engineers worked night and day during these atrocious conditions and overcame almost insurmountable difficulties. In addition to the weather, the bridge sites were continually under artillery fire or subjected to bombing.

The Chief Engineer of Third Army, Brigadier General John F. Conklin and his executive officer, Colonel David H. Tulley, were on the job continually, supervising the construction work, as were of course the commanding officers of the various combat engineer battalions. General Patton also visited the crossings frequently, especially if they were having a particularly difficult time. Sometimes, where it was taking too long to build a bridge, our tanks, guns and men were ferried across rivers.

At this time it was announced that two spies, caught behind our lines, were executed by Third Army.

After crossing the Seille River our troops passed beyond several 7th Armored Division tanks which had been shot up by the Germans back in the latter part of September before the restraining line had been laid down for Third Army. Bodies of a number of American dead still remained in these tanks six or seven weeks later.

When our medics, and quartermasters of the Graves Registration Section, undertook to remove these bodies, they found that they had been booby trapped. It was just another act of sheer wanton barbarity on the part of the Heinies, typical of them and their training. For while there were a few casualties from the booby traps caused among our men, it did not directly help the German cause a great deal, for the casualties were among the medical and quartermaster men.

Another German trick was leaving time bombs in buildings. These really did cause a great many casualties among our troops as they were very effective. Because of the constant bad weather buildings wherever possible were used for shelter. These time bombs were concealed so ingeniously in the walls and under the floors of buildings that they were almost impossible to discover. Often they were buried deep in the foundations and covered over with cement. They could be set for periods up to 21 days. In the 80th Division especially they caused large numbers of killed and wounded. In several cases, many days after the enemy had been driven out, whole buildings blew up and nothing was left of them but a pile of rubble.

By mid-November the Germans had reinforced in our front with several more divisions—the 21st Panzer Division, from the Seventh Army front; the 25th Panzer Grenadier Division; the 553d Infantry Division; the 35th Infantry Division and the 106th Panzer Brigade.

Our G-2 estimated that there were now the equivalent of at least eight divisions along our front with 285 tanks or assault guns. The enemy, however, was using all types of soldiers. A P.W. from the 11th Panzer Division stated that he had been in the army less than four months; another one had a glass eye; another a partially restored face; and still another was a convalescent just returned from the hospital.

During these days of bitter fighting the low ceiling frequently made it difficult or impossible for our air corps to give much close support to our ground troops.

In the XX Corps zone, while the 95th and the 5th Infantry Divisions continued to press toward the heart of Metz from the north and south, the 90th Infantry Division, preceded by Task Force Polk, continued to push further east in the northern sector, and the 10th Armored Division, in the south, was thrusting way beyond Metz toward the German border.

By 18 November our infantry patrols had entered the outskirts of Metz and we had captured the airfield on the south of the town. Our troops were now encountering new types of mines which were almost impossible to detect—they were plastic and wooden mines, which our mine detectors could not pick up.

At this time the Allied radio reported that Himmler had taken over supreme command from Hitler's faltering hands. It was pointed out that this meant, even more than ever, fighting to the last man. It was stated that Hitler's paranoia made it impossible for him to continue to govern.

On the 18th the weather cleared somewhat, and our air had one of its best days in some time. There was a tremendous amount of enemy rail activity observed in the Third Army front. This was probably because the poor flying weather in the past two and a half weeks had given the Germans time to repair their railroads. Seventy-three moving trains were noted, not counting 33% to 100% activity in the marshalling yards. Two hundred seventy-five locomotives and 1100 railroad cars were noted. All of this activity was west of the Rhine.

On the 19th of November also there were heavy road movements of German troops east of Metz but they were screened by smoke. Two more forts surrendered on this day, Forts Flappeville and St. Julien, leaving five of the principle ones still holding out—Verdun, Driant, Jeanne d'Arc, Derouledge and Gambetta and a few smaller ones like Privat and Quelen. At Fort Bellecroix there was a tremendous explosion that sounded as though they were demolishing their installations.

By the 20th our forces had penetrated to the center of the city of Metz and bitter street fighting ensued with the SS troops and the volkstorm troops there.

By 21 November the XII Corps in the south had captured Dieuze, Morhange and Faulquimont, and on the same date in the XX Corps zone in the north, all organized resistance in Metz ceased, although there continued to be some sniping and the five forts mentioned were still holding out. The 10th Armored Division and Task Force Polk were fighting inside Germany, at several points at this time, far to the east.

One of the groups which had fought hardest in Metz had been the students in an Officers Candidate School, in the city. There had been several hundreds of them and they were fanatical and desperate fighters. As Third Army troops closed in on the city, each one of the instructors of the school was ordered to take 20 or 30 of these students with him to defend a certain sector and to fight to the bitter end. No second order was necessary to these fanatical youngsters, and they caused hundreds of casualties among our troops. It was only toward the very end that any of them surrendered, and then only one or two at a time.

A day or two after the organized fighting ceased I entered the city from the south over the one road that was then open. It was a most interesting experience. On the way north we passed through the flooded country and through the half destroyed, deserted villages, where dead horses and cattle and once in awhile the body of a dead soldier or civilian were strewn around. Most of the civilian inhabitants had not started to straggle back as yet. Concrete pillboxes and dugouts with log tops could be seen through the woods and in the hills where the Heinies had established defense lines, and the more permanent Maginot forts were seen here and there. We passed through many road blocks and saw where the Krauts had dynamited the trees at critical points to fell them across the roads to slow up our advancing troops. In many places were smashed tanks and guns and at one point where a dead horse was lying still harnessed to a destroyed gun, there stood a live horse with all his harness on, but both the traces were broken and dangling on the ground. American shells had apparently smashed the German gun and killed one horse and the other one had broken the traces and run away. It had now come back to its mate and was standing there forlornly beside it.

In several places in the fields we saw wooden German tanks which had been placed in various locations to fool us as to the enemy's real strength and to mislead us and cause us to waste our artillery fire. These wooden tanks were quite a good imitation from a distance, and were built over farm wagon frames so that they could be hauled from place to place.

As we entered the city we saw that it was badly shot up and filthy. During the seige the water supply had been demolished and garbage and rubbish and other litter were piled everywhere. This was in addition to all the stones, bricks, glass, etc. caused by the bombing and shelling. Scarcely any German civilians remained, but there were plenty of dead soldiers around and our tanks were rumbling through the streets. As mentioned, several forts surrounding the city were still holding out, and were frequently dropping artillery shells inside the city itself. Our tanks and artillery were firing from the inside onto these forts to keep them covered and to prevent them, as far as possible, from firing.

We visited an infantry battalion of the 5th Infantry Division which was containing Fort Privat and was close to the southern edge of town. The battalion commander took us to a forward observation post in the loft of a small barn. A shell from the fort had torn a hole through the roof and through it we could plainly see every detail of the fort only a couple of hundred yards away as well as the helmets of our doughboys in their foxholes just ahead of us.

The tactics of this battalion commander were interesting and were rather typical of the way all of the forts were finally reduced. The doughboys were sent forward at night, to almost the base of the fort, to dig foxholes in which they remained all the next day. Just before daylight each morning a new group of doughboys, after having been fed a hot meal, went out to relieve those in the foxholes. They carried K rations with them for the noon meal and after dark that evening hot food was taken down to them. All during the day and night, tanks and machine guns, located at strategic points, kept firing on all sides of the fort, and the doughboys fired on anything that moved or that made the slightest noise at night.

Thus the Heinies were kept almost entirely underground and only occasionally were able to fire. Each fort was kept contained that way until one by one they ran out of food and water and their morale went lower and lower until they finally surrendered. But it was a long process. Fort Privat did not surrender till 30 November.

By 25 November the XII Corps was closing in on the Saar Valley and the 4th Armored Division, followed closely by the 26th and 35th Infantry Divisions, was crossing the Saar River.

By the 29th of November XX Corps also had three divisions pushing into Germany near Saarlautern—the 10th Armored, the 90th and the 95th Infantry. Five of the Metz Forts were still holding out although most of the corps was now twenty-five miles to the east of Metz.

At this time a new task force was formed in the vicinity of St. Avold, which had been former headquarters of the Gestapo. It was composed of the 6th Cavalry Group Headquarters and 6th Cavalry Squadron, a Ranger Battalion, a tank destroyer company and a combat engineer company. It was named Task Force Fickett after the commander of the 6th Cavalry—Colonel E. M. "Fighting Joe" Fickett, as he was called. "Fighting Joe" did some excellent work here and also later in the Battle of the Bulge.

On 2 December our air reported a number of convoys on the roads in Germany. These convoys were about 50% military and 50% civilian refugees. The tables were now beginning to be turned on Hitler's "supermen." These were Herrenvolk refugees being driven from their homes as we got inside Germany, not Poles or French or Czechs.

A town in France was burned and completely destroyed by the Germans as they retreated. This was in line with an enemy document captured a few days previously, which ordered all buildings destroyed which could be used as cover for our troops. We interpreted it, however, as an indication that the enemy did not expect to counterattack in this Saar area. (This information and the conclusion drawn were valuable a little later, when General Patton suddenly withdrew most of his forces from this sector and rushed them north, to attack the southern flank of Von Rundstedt's Ardennes offensive.)

In the Metz area, on 5 December, three of the forts still continued to hold out. P.W.'s, however, reported morale within the forts was getting very low. One commanding officer ordered his men to fire 1,000 rounds of ammunition every day regardless of targets, indicating that as soon as the ammunition was all gone, there would be no use fighting any longer, and they could surrender with honor.

On 6 December a new Corps Headquarters, the III Corps, commanded by Major General John Millikin, which had been assigned to Third Army, was established in Metz. While its units were assembling, the mission assigned it was the final reduction of the remaining forts around Metz while the XX Corps moved further east behind its advancing troops.

At this time our G-2 stated in his report that the enemy strategic reserves along the western front were between 20 and 30 divisions.

On this same day, the Third Army liberated 29 French towns. Since the beginning of this operation on 8 November, the Third Army had liberated 836 towns. Our shells were now dropping on Saarbrucken and we had a 30 mile wide breach through the Siegfried Line across the Saar River. Most of Saarguemines was in our hands and there was street fighting in Dillingen.

On this date, 6 December, the Allied invasion was just six months old. During that time, all of France; all of Belgium; all of Luxembourg and most of Holland had been liberated.

On 7 December—press and radio announced that it was the third anniversary of Pearl Harbor; the church bells would ring and there would be several moments of silence in memory of those who had been killed.

The bitterest kind of fighting was taking place all along our front and many German counter-attacks were being made. An estimated 6,000 rounds of enemy artillery shells fell in the vicinity of Saarbrucken alone on one day. Our bridges were under fire all day and all night long.

More time bombs in buildings and culverts behind our lines were exploding every day causing casualties to our troops. Whole buildings would collapse without warning, and in a culvert under a road near Les Stangs, a crater was suddenly blown 20 feet wide, 15 feet deep and an estimated 150 feet long.

At one point as our troops advanced they freed 1700 French civilians who were being held prisoner in caves ready to be evacuated to Germany.

The 12th Army Group reported more German divisions from Norway were continuing to arrive in Denmark on the way to the front. They were all good, well-trained divisions. Some were SS divisions.

On 9 December Fort Driant fell.

Snow 6 inches or more fell along most of the First Army front.

On this same day in Saarbrucken a fight took place in a pottery factory which was reminiscent of a bar room brawl. Americans and Germans were climbing over machinery and benches, machine gunning and throwing grenades and pottery at each other. The Heinies were finally driven out of the factory.

On 14 December, Fort Jeanne d'Arc, the last of the Metz forts, finally capitulated. When it fell, although it originally had several thousand troops in it, only 514 P.W.'s were captured, including 13 officers and 3 civilians. The balance had either been killed or had escaped by infiltrating out of the fort during the long weeks of its seige.

On 15 December G-2 stated that in the northern sector of the XX Corps patrols during the night reported active and heavy movements of tanks and other vehicles in the enemy rear areas.

In the bridgehead area across the Saar there continued the bitterest house to house and pillbox fighting. In one enemy counter-attack 85 Germans charged the front lines shouting "Heil Hitler"! They were all annihilated.

During this month Brigadier General Edward T. Williams, the artillery officer of the Third Army had a practice demonstration with a new secret weapon. It was a radar operated proximity fuse on artillery shells. Instead of exploding the shell on contact or by a time device, this new fuse exploded it by means of a radar beam which traveled from the nose of the shell to the earth or solid object which the shell approached in its flight. The ray was immediately returned from the earth or solid object to the nose of the shell, and caused the shell to explode about 20 yards from the object it was approaching. In this way the full blast of the shell and the flying splinters became effective against ground troops. It was also excellent in antiaircraft guns firing at aircraft.

In the test demonstration of this fuse the results were almost perfect. Shells of various sizes were fired in battery and battalion concentrations in a section of terrain full of hills and valleys. As the shells with this radar fuse fell on this irregular ground, it was interesting to see the bursts take place at approximately 20 yards above the earth, whether they fell on high ground or low. General Patton was greatly pleased, but ordered these fuzes kept very secret and in reserve to use against the Germans at a critical time as a surprise to them, so that the greatest damaging effect could be attained. It was not necessary to wait very long for this time.

It was now past the middle of December. The fortress of Metz and its surrounding forts had all been subdued. Through the most stubbornly defended country and against the strongest sector of the Siegfried Line, in atrocious rainy and winter weather, our troops had driven 50 miles or more and had crossed the Saar River in three or four places and established through the Siegfried Line on the soil of Germany, a 30 mile wedge or bridgehead. The Third Army was now ready to capitalize on this, and General Patton was having plans prepared for an all-out push to the Rhine. The plans were in course of preparation in our G-3 Operations Section, and our G-4 was bringing up the necessary supplies. This all-out offensive to the east through our wedge in the Siegfried Line was scheduled to commence on 21 December.

Something happened just north of Third Army sector, however, which prevented this planned offensive.

12

Battle of the Bulge

THE Grand Duchy of Luxembourg is one of the most attractive and beautiful of the small countries of Europe. It is a triangle, with Germany bordering it on the east and northeast, France on the south and Belgium on the west and northwest.

Because it is so tiny and is surrounded by larger and more powerful and aggressive neighbors, its people are linguists. Besides their own language, Luxembourgers speak French, German, Flemish, one of the languages of Belgium, and many of them are fluent in English. English is taught in the schools and most of the better class have a good command of it. Walking along the city streets, small children often would take us by the hand and chatter away in English. They are a cosmopolitan and friendly people. Although there is no tremendous wealth, before the war they were prosperous and there was no poverty in the whole country.

During the stay of Third Army Headquarters in the city of Luxembourg we met and talked to dozens of the people of the city and many were the stories we heard about the treatment during the German occupation. One of the most vivid stories I heard from a young American woman who had married a Luxembourg doctor. She was the daughter of a Harvard professor and had met her husband on a trip to Europe after her graduation from Vassar. She and her husband and three children had lived in Echternach, a beautiful little resort-town on

137

the banks of the Saur River opposite the Siegfried Line in Germany. Her husband had been taken back into Germany as a hostage when the Heinies retreated in September. Their home had been wrecked by artillery shells, and after the Von Runstedt offensive commenced in December, this young woman and her three children had been forced to live in cellars among the rubble and had been fed by troops of the 4th Infantry Division, which held the town during the battle. At the time I talked to her she and her children had been evacuated to the city of Luxembourg.

She told me the story of the first German invasion of Luxembourg on 10 May 1940:

For about two weeks before the invasion they could see the German troops collecting in the town directly across the river from Echternach. At night they could plainly hear them singing—one of their favorite songs being "Roll out the Barrel." The Luxembourgers had placed token log-barriers across the bridges from Germany, but they were entirely undefended as they had no army whatsoever.

On the morning of 10 May, the inhabitants of Echternach were wakened by much noise and loud cheering on the other side of the river, and about 0900 the German columns started across through the log barriers against no opposition.

An elderly woman, a patient of the doctor, this young woman's husband, had just come out of the doctor's office and descended the steps from their house, as the German armored columns dashed across the bridge and through the town. She had just reached the side walk as the armored cars and tanks came along the street, and stood on the curb not sure just where to go. On the sidewalks on each side of the columns came columns of German motorcycle troops, and one of these deliberately hit this elderly woman and knocked her forward, face first, into the street and a tank ran over her, crushing her to death. And all day long, my informant told me, the body lay there as tank after tank ran over it until it was unrecognizable as a human body.

German troops remained in the town for several days and any demand made on a civilian had to be obeyed instantly. A German soldier, seeing a man walking toward his home one day with a piece of ham and a loaf of bread under his arm, demanded that the food be turned over to him. When the man demurred for an instant, the German whipped out his pistol and shot him dead, leaving his body lying in the street as an example to other civilians.

The population of the Grand Duchy before the war was around 300,000. The police force numbered 300, including 60 in the army, which was merely a guard for the palace of the Grand Duchess. However, the Germans took 60,000 prisoners with them into Germany and kept them as hostages for the good behavior of the country during the German occupation. Many of them were used as slave labor in Germany. I talked with several of these after they were liberated and returned to Luxembourg. I also talked to dozens of families in which one or more members had been carried into Germany. Almost every family had lost one or more this way. Some had heard from their relatives either directly or through the underground, but some had heard nothing for more than four years. About half of the hostages had been taken away at the beginning of the war, the balance just before the Americans entered in September, 1944.

The countryside everywhere was beautiful and rolling, with hills and valleys, streams and lakes, and an abundance of trees, especially rich, dark evergreens on the hillsides. The cities and towns were attractive, artistic and clean. The farms were well kept and prosperous looking, and a network of excellent roads linked the towns and villages.

Luxembourg, capital city of the Grand Duchy of the same name, is a beautifully laid out place of 60,000 population. It seems much larger because of its wide streets and fine, large buildings. The city lies on the tops of several high hills separated by deep canyons formed by the beautiful, winding Alzette River and its main tributary, the Petrusse. Many buildings have been erected down the steep sides of these gorges and magnificent parks run along the river banks at the bottom. The city has parks through all sections of its upper levels, where most of the fine buildings are located. One may reach all parts of the upper city by means of stone arched bridges, the full width of the roads. These massive old stone arches and the stately old and new buildings with their high-pitched, French tile roofs and towers, make you think of the scenery in the old musical comedy, "The Chocolate Soldier."

The city of Luxembourg in early days was called the "Bastion of the North." It was built as a fortress and walled city to defend against the Huns and to prevent them from overflowing toward the south into France. Under the city, built in the rock and earth of the hilltops, there are today 80 miles of underground passages. These were originally intended to shelter the inhabitants when they were attacked and to rush troops from one end of the city to the other to repel attackers.

I had visited Luxembourg one day in September when the 12th Army Group Headquarters moved in, just after it had been captured by the First Army. The city had not been badly damaged, as the Germans had retreated rapidly. I had lunch at the Hotel Brasseur, still operating, and which had been the headquarters of a German Gestapo general and his staff.

After lunch, the hotel manager told me of the German evacuation. He said that almost two weeks before the 5th Armored Division arrived, the Germans became panic-stricken and pulled out in a hurry, leaving most of their baggage and their girl companions. When our troops did not arrive immediately, they all came back and set up again in the hotel.

Then one day shortly after noon, they were all sitting in the big dining room when suddenly overhead, flying low, came a group of 16 or 18 planes. They could be plainly seen through the windows and all the Germans rushed over for a look. Then they started jabbering in German: "They are Americans! They are Americans!" There was great excitement and confusion. They dashed up to their rooms, threw their baggage together and hustled away to Germany, accompanied this time by their girl friends, just as the firing of the 5th Armored Division was heard as it entered the upper end of the town.

The hotel manager told me that the reception the inhabitants gave our troops was simply beyond description. I could well believe it, for I knew what we had received all through France.

Little did I realize that day in late September that in December, during the von Rundstedt offensive, this same Hotel Brasseur would become the officers' mess and quarters for the senior officers of Third Army Headquarters.

As mentioned in the previous chapter, on 16 December, Third Army Headquarters was still in Nancy, France. Plans were being perfected there by General Patton for his all-out dash through the Siegfried Line, projected for 21 December. A new headquarters location was being set up for Third Army at St. Avold, France, near the German border.

Our XII Corps was still on the south of the Third Army front, with the 35th Division and a new infantry division, the 87th, in the line and the 4th Armored and 80th Infantry drawn back in reserve.

The III Corps had just taken over a sector of our front

in the center, with the 26th Infantry Division, Task Force Fickett and the 6th Armored Division.

In the north part of our front was the XX Corps with the 90th and 95th Infantry Divisions and the 10th Armored Division and the 3d Cavalry Group in the line, and the 5th Infantry Division in the rear, reorganizing after the bitter battle for Metz.

And then the big news developed in the north, in the front of the First Army, which upset all calculations for a while on the Western Front.

We first heard of it on 16 December, when our Liaison Officer from the First Army told us that the VIII Corps had been heavily counterattacked in the Ardennes sector that day and was forced to give some ground. There also was heavy fighting on the V Corps front, a little farther north. Counterattacks there had been repulsed but no change in that front was reported.

The Ninth Bomber Command was unable to operate because of the weather, but the XIX Tactical Air Force reported extensive rail activity in the Trier area in Germany behind the lines, and much road convoy activity. Seven squadrons of our XIX Tactical Air Force were ordered to assist on the VIII Corps front of the First Army the next day.

On 17 December, G-2 reported that the focal point of the enemy activity was in the northern sector of the VIII Corps. This activity, however, soon spread all along the VIII Corps front. Some enemy penetrations had been made and some towns captured. On this one day 12 new divisional identifications were made on VIII Corps front, eight infantry and four Panzer divisions. There now were 16 divisions making the attack in VIII Corps area alone, with an estimated 280 tanks.

That night the Luftwaffe was active along the whole front, strafing and bombing. There also were reports that many parachutists were being dropped behind our lines. A prisoner taken by the VIII Corps said three additional divisions were training where his division had trained and were scheduled to attack. The 46th Volksgrenadier Division, which was considered to have been fairly well destroyed several weeks before and had been withdrawn from the line, was again identified, all three regiments of it—a masterful piece of reorganization in a short time.

The few observation planes which could observe the next day reported continued heavy rail and road movements in the vicinity of Trier and Homburg. Several road convoys ten miles long were seen. These were hit by our planes and in several cases heavy explosions followed, indicating they apparently were heavy ammunition supply columns. One enemy concentration of 200 vehicles was attacked by air and scattered.

It should be remembered that for weeks before von Rundstedt launched his great offensive, the weather had been bad for flying and of course for observation. It had rained incessantly, the skies were overcast and there had been a persistent ground mist. The weather had now become colder and a heavy snow had blanketed most of the First Army front, which didn't help the situation.

When the German attack started, VIII Corps Headquarters was at Bastogne and the Corps front was about 90 miles long. It was held by only three infantry divisions, the 4th in the south, the 28th in the center and the 106th in the north. These three, plus the 9th Armored and the 101st Airborne, which were brought in as reserves, bore the brunt of the German attack. Of these, the 4th Infantry and the 28th (Keystone) Divisions had been badly mauled in the battle of the Hurtgen Forest and had been withdrawn for rest to what had been considered a quiet front. The 106th was a new division with only ten days combat experience.

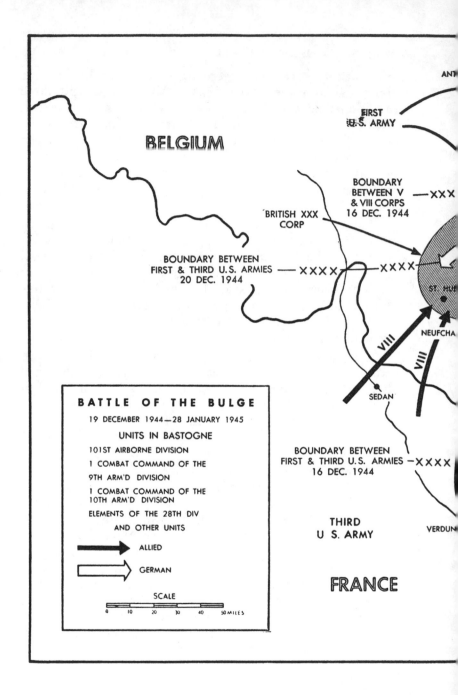

BELGIUM

ANT

FIRST
U.S. ARMY

BOUNDARY
BETWEEN V — XXX
& VIII CORPS
16 DEC. 1944

BRITISH XXX
CORP

BOUNDARY BETWEEN
FIRST & THIRD U.S. ARMIES — XXXX ——— XXXX
20 DEC. 1944

ST. HU

NEUFCHA

VIII

VIII

SEDAN

BOUNDARY BETWEEN
FIRST & THIRD U.S. ARMIES — XXXX
16 DEC. 1944

THIRD   VERDUN
U S. ARMY

FRANCE

BATTLE OF THE BULGE

19 DECEMBER 1944—28 JANUARY 1945

UNITS IN BASTOGNE

101ST AIRBORNE DIVISION

1 COMBAT COMMAND OF THE
9TH ARM'D DIVISION

1 COMBAT COMMAND OF THE
10TH ARM'D DIVISION

ELEMENTS OF THE 28TH DIV

AND OTHER UNITS

➤ ALLIED

⇨ GERMAN

SCALE

0   10   20   30   40   50 MILES

No one can fully realize the fury of that blow. It was well conceived and masterfully executed by von Rundstedt, who was considered one of the brainiest of the German high commanders. It was a bold and desperate stroke and it almost worked. If it had, the whole history of the war might have been changed.

Von Rundstedt's plan was to strike swiftly at the weakest point in our line, very much as we had done at St. Lo in Normandy. If our line could be pierced, then he could drive all of his reserves through, capture Liege and Antwerp—our largest base and port—completely separate our armies in the north and south, and possibly destroy one or both of them by coming up in the rear and cutting off their supply lines.

This was exactly what General Patton had done when he pushed his whole Third Army through the gap at Avranches, then spread out over the whole of France and finally came up behind the German Seventh Army, opposite the British, the Canadians and the First U. S. Army, to form the Falaise Pocket.

It is an interesting fact that in the Ardennes offensive, or "Battle of the Bulge," as it is popularly called, von Rundstedt used 23 divisions, eight panzers and fifteen infantry. In the breakthrough at St. Lo, the Americans had not used nearly so many. When General Patton pushed his Third Army through the eight-mile-wide gap at Avranches, it was composed of only 12 divisions—five armored and seven infantry. The German divisional strength at this time was not as great as ours, but the total number of German troops used in von Rundstedt's drive was probably greater than ours at St. Lo and Avranches.

Their equipment also was excellent. Their Tiger and Panther tanks and their 88-mm guns were better than ours although each division probably did not have the total number of tanks and guns that ours had.

They also had in their favor experienced and battle-hardened veterans, while at Avranches many of our divisions were committed to battle for the first time. The German divisions in the Ardennes were all veteran divisions, which had been re-equipped, rested and trained. Many of them had had experience on the Russian front and in Norway, and they were the best that Germany had. Some were Elite SS Divisions.

They had all been primed for this great drive. When they first came through they had American-speaking men in each unit. As they charged into our lines, they yelled at the top of their lungs and over loud speakers, in English, calling our soldiers every foul and filthy name they could and using every curse word in our American vocabulary. This, of course, was an attempt to intimidate our troops. They came over in wave after wave of tanks, infantry and self-propelled guns and in trucks, yelling and firing. At first they took no prisoners, but killed our boys who did surrender, as in the case of the 150 men of an artillery observation battalion, who were overrun on the road, captured and immediately lined up in a field and mowed down in cold blood by machine guns.

Our men reported that the Germans apparently were "hopped up" with dope. Many of them were half mad and under the influence of liquor.

One of the plans of the Germans was to capture our stores of food, ammunition and gasoline, which would help them continue their drive. In this they were partly successful at first. Several hundred of our artillery pieces and trucks were captured intact, and thousands of rounds of our ammunition were turned against us from our own guns.

At its maximum the German drive opened a breach in our lines 80 miles wide and their armor penetrated to a depth of 50 miles. There was nothing ahead of them but open country. But on the flanks of this opening they had to cope with forces that moved even faster than they did.

To the everlasting credit of our fighting men and their officers of the VIII Corps, although thinly scattered and outnumbered at first by ten to one, they stood up to this German onslaught and gave blow for blow. History has already written the results of this bloodiest of the battles of this war, but the thousands of individual deeds of heroism will never be told. There were too many of them. As the Germans advanced, drunk and doped and full of false confidence instilled in them by years of propaganda about the super-race, our plain American men, practical and unassuming but confident, slugged it out with them. For three days our three infantry divisions, the 4th, 28th and 106th, slowed up the German power drive and, reinforced by the 9th Armored Division, the 101st Airborne Division and one combat command of the 10th Armored Division, held the 23 German divisions until help could arrive.

By 18 December the enemy was continuing his attack in the northern sector of the VIII Corps, and the southern sector of the V Corps had been penetrated to a depth of 12 miles. Two regiments of the 106th Division had been isolated and completely surrounded. The 28th was being heavily pressed and had been penetrated by five or six miles. In the southern sector of VIII Corps the enemy had penetrated several miles and fighting was going on in the town of Echternach along the Sauer River on the German border.

On this day the Eighth Air Force, the Ninth Bomber Command and the RAF were all grounded by the weather. The tactical air forces, however, went up despite the weather and had one of the busiest days of the month. They claimed 120 enemy planes destroyed in the air, against a loss of 32 of ours. The XIX Tactical was extremely busy on both the Third Army and the VIII Corps fronts. At one point our close-support air broke up a concentration of 400 to 500 enemy vehicles. It was estimated that on the First Army front alone on this day, the enemy had in the air between 400 and 500 planes, 100 or more on the Ninth Army front to the north of First Army, and were active also on the Third and Seventh Army fronts. They were putting practically everything they had into this drive.

G-2 on this day reported that the chief enemy activity was in the south sector of the V Corps and the north sector of the VIII Corps of First Army. For the first time the attack was proclaimed a "Major Enemy Effort"!. One-half of the Sixth Panzer Army had already been identified. Penetrations had been made from three to four miles on the V Corps front and 12 miles on the VIII Corps front. The attack in the south, near Echternach, on the southern hinge, was against the 4th Infantry Division, which was holding fairly firm.

On the Third Army front there was considerable enemy activity, especially in the northern part of the XX Corps. Enemy reinforcements were being brought in and there were heavy rail movements east of Kaiserslautern. Night fighters all reported extremely heavy night movements behind the enemy lines on the roads and rails. German prisoners said the enemy was being heavily reinforced. Enemy artillery had been reinforced and was much more active. Quantities of smoke shells were being fired and many high burst adjustments indicated he was preparing for further attacks. Much construction was heard at river and stream crossings, which the enemy attempted to conceal by the noise of small arms fire.

Up to this time all announcements about the German attack had come from the American side. Berlin had said nothing of it as yet. On the First Army front, fighting continued all night. Many paratroopers were dropped and the Luftwaffe was up in force.

On the morning of 19 December no regular briefing was held in the war room of Third Army Headquarters.

A special meeting was called by General Patton, however, to be held at 0800 in the office of Brigadier General H. G. Maddox, G-3. Those present, in addition to the General and his staff, were the Corps Commanders with their G-3's and Artillery Officers.

General Patton told us that the situation with the First Army was serious but not alarming. The Germans had made a major breakthrough to a depth of 15 to 20 miles in the north sector of the VIII Corps and the south sector of the V Corps, First Army.

One whole U. S. division—the 106th—had been decimated, the 28th Division had been badly battered and one Combat Command of the 9th Armored had been practically destroyed. The VIII Corps Headquarters had been forced to flee and no one knew exactly where it was at that time. Enemy armor and infantry had penetrated to within a half mile of the First Army command post, forcing its withdrawal.

General Patton said that the preceding day he had met at Luxembourg with General Bradley and had talked with General Eisenhower by telephone. The situation was very fluid but, in general, the Third Army had been ordered to be prepared to turn on its axis and attack to the north. He, General Patton, was to attend another meeting with General Eisenhower and General Bradley at Verdun at 0930 that morning, but he desired the staff to know as much of the plan as possible so they could be thinking along new lines and working out details while he was gone.

The general plan, which of course was subject to change and confirmation after the meeting at Verdun, was as follows:

The XII Corps, presently holding the south sector of Third Army and composed of the 35th and 87th Infantry and 4th Armored Divisions, might be ordered to extend to the north and take over all the present Third

Army front. In all probability the Seventh Army would be asked to extend its front to the north, relieving the XII Corps of part of the front, or else the XV Corps might be assigned to Third Army to help hold the front. Meantime, the 6th Army Group, south of Third Army, had been ordered to go on the defensive. It was expected that the 12th Armored division of the Seventh Army would be assigned soon to the Third Army.

General Eddy, commanding the XII Corps, was told to place one combat command of the 4th Armored Division in reserve, in a strategic position in the rear so that it could strike in any direction.

The XX Corps, composed of the 5th, 90th and 95th Infantry Divisions, was to be prepared to move in a northeasterly direction.

The III Corps, composed of the 26th and 80th Infantry and 6th Armored Divisions, was to be prepared to move in a northerly direction on the left flank of the XX Corps.

He added that in all probability the VIII Corps Headquarters, if it had not been destroyed, would be placed under the Third Army, as well as what was left of the 4th and 28th Infantry and 9th Armored Divisions.

The Third Army zone would be everything south of Bastogne, former location of VIII Corps Headquarters, down to our present southern army boundary.

General Patton told General Eddy to hold his present front lines, if possible, and not to go back to the Maginot Line forts unless it was unavoidable as he, General Patton, had not abandoned his plans for an eventual breakthrough of the Siegfried Line on that front and meant to resume them as soon as possible.

Colonel Koch, G-2, pointed out that there were strong indications that at least two new enemy divisions and possibly more had unloaded in our immediate front within the past two days.

General Maddox, G-3, gave the latest information on the enemy breakthrough and said the First Army was burning gasoline stores and destroying other supplies as it retreated.

In addition to these officers, General Muller, G-4; Colonel Nixon, Ordnance; and General Williams, Artillery Officer, gave details of the situation in regard to their branches and the Corps Commanders also made statements or asked questions. General Williams requested that General Patton release the new Radar fuse, the automatic radar air-burst fuse, for use, and General Patton said this would be permitted upon Corps order. General Weyland, XIX Tactical Air Force commander, also was consulted.

After the meeting, General Maddox instructed me as Chief Liaison Officer to send an officer to try to locate VIII Corps Headquarters. Major Wolf was immediately dispatched.

Then General Patton left for his meeting at Verdun with Generals Eisenhower and Bradley. At that meeting General Eisenhower asked Patton "How many days he would need to wheel the Third Army north to the assistance of the First".

General Patton grinned at the Supreme Allied Commander as he replied: "Days, hell! We're already on the way!"

Colonel Paul Harkins, Deputy Chief of Staff, who accompanied General Patton to Verdun, telephoned back to headquarters to arrange a special meeting of the Chiefs of Section of Third Army Headquarters as soon as the General returned late that afternoon.

At that meeting General Patton spoke as follows:

"Gentlemen, this is a hell of a Christmas present, but it was handed to me and I pass it on to you. Tonight the Third Army turns and attacks to the north. I would have much preferred to have continued our attack to the east as planned, but I am a soldier. I fight where I am told, and I win where I fight! There is one encouraging factor in our favor, however. The b------s will be easier to kill coming at us above ground than they would be skulking in their holes. You have all done a grand job so far, but I expect more of you now".

That was General Patton's call to battle—a battle that literally shortened the war by months and that saved Luxembourg and Belgium, possibly France, from being overrun once more by the enemy.

The staff meeting broke up and each Section Chief went to his job, for each knew exactly what he had to do. It was no easy task for most of our divisions to break off contact with the enemy in the east and, cutting directly across our own supply lines, crash head-on into the flank of an onrushing enemy. The weather did not help, either, for there not only was rain and mud, but snow, sleet and fog, as well.

General Patton ordered a thin defensive screen of some infantry and cavalry units to be used to hold the front against the Germans in the east, and the bulk of his army of approximately 300,000 troops started to plow north over the slippery, congested roads. The 80th Infantry Division had been put in trucks and it and the 4th Armored already were on the roads headed north. Inside of 48 hours the bulk of the Third Army was driving north and attacking the south flank of the Belgian Bulge. Our units traveled from 50 to 150 miles in the most impossible winter conditions. It was, without doubt, the fastest and greatest mass movement of an army in history.

Von Rundstedt, the German Field Marshal, after his capture on May 4th, just before the German final surrender, stated:

"The counteroffensive in the Ardennes last December would have succeeded if supplies and reserves could have been brought up as quickly as General Patton moved up from the south."

General Patton's warning order had been altered slightly after the meeting at Verdun, for XX Corps remained on the east front, and III and XII Corps were ordered north to attack Von Rundstedt's southern flank. VIII Corps, as had been expected, reverted to Third Army.

On 20 December, the morning after the dash north was started, an advance detachment of Third Army Headquarters moved from Nancy to the city of Luxembourg. I was fortunate enough to be ordered to go with it. Besides General Patton there were 35 officers and 60 enlisted men. From Nancy to Luxembourg by road is about 100 miles. The roads were jammed with our tanks and trucks moving swiftly north but, in my jeep, I arrived shortly before noon and reported to 12th Army Group Headquarters to find out where General Bradley wanted us to set up our headquarters.

An officer at 12th Army Group Headquarters invited me to lunch with him at their senior officers' mess. As we entered the dining room of one of the hotels, used for the mess, eight or ten officers, some of whom I did not even know, came over to shake hands with me and said: "We sure are glad to see you. You will have lunch with us, won't you?" As I had already accepted one invitation, I gladly agreed. But they all, having seen the Third Army patch on my shoulder, added one more question: "Where are the rest of you? When will they be here?"

Never before had I realized the really great power in a name—the name of General Patton. Driving through the streets of Luxembourg on that dull, cold December day, the sidewalks were filled with civilians. Their faces were drawn and haggard with worry. Their jaws sagged and there were no smiles, for they were scared—scared that the hated Germans might return. They knew that the enemy was only six or seven miles away and still driving on. The guns could be heard plainly, rumbling off to the north.

All the American flags I had seen decorating the streets and hanging from the windows when I visited the city in September had disappeared. Not one was in sight. And the signs "We speak English" on store windows were being removed. I did not blame these people. They had experienced the hell of being conquered by the Germans. But as so often happens at a sad or serious time, I suddenly remembered the remark of a friend when we first crossed the border into the Grand Duchy. Across the road in large letters were the words: "Welcome to our Liberators". My friend had said, jokingly: "What this little country needs, surrounded as it is by powerful countries on all sides, is a revolving sign at each of its borders, to say in English, German, French and Belgian, 'Welcome to our Liberators'. Then, just by a twirl of the sign, the right welcome could be flashed."

There was intense excitement on the streets of Luxembourg that day, and great crowds were out. But when the word spread, as it did by the middle of the afternoon, that General Patton and his Third Army were on the roll north, and as our armored and infantry columns in trucks came rumbling through the streets in unbroken columns, the effect was electric.

Many of the Luxembourgers, as I have said, spoke English. They would ask the tank drivers and the doughboys in the trucks: "General Patton? Third Army?" And when the answer would come back: "Yes, General Patton's Third Army", their faces would lose their tenseness, worried looks disappeared and they smiled, laughed and even cheered. It was as though an electric current had sent a thrilling shock through the whole community. I had never seen anything like it in my life.

There was great excitement all that day. Third Army Headquarters was to be set up in a large school building, which had been cleared and assigned to us. After visiting it, I returned to 12th Army Group Headquarters to con-

fer about something. As I attempted to enter the drive-
way to the big building, I was brusquely halted by a
young sentry and told to take my jeep out immediately.
Since I had been there only an hour or so before and had
been entertained at lunch, I was quite perturbed and
asked the sentry what the h--- was the matter with him,
that I had my identification card, etc.

He was all excited and told me to have my car backed
out at once or he would shoot, and he stepped back,
pulled the bolt on his rifle and aimed it at me. I was a bit
taken aback, and couldn't understand this treatment, when
they had all been so glad to see me from Third Army such
a short time before.

Then a sergeant of the guard came running up and told
me the only way I could get in now was to go across the
street to a telephone, call the officer I wanted to see and
have him come out of the headquarters, identify me and
take me in with him. I then saw that extra sentries were
at the alert all around the headquarters building.

I still couldn't imagine what had caused the change, but
just then Colonel Hammond, Chief Signal Officer of
Third Army, came up and explained that word had been
flashed that the Germans the night before had dropped a
large number of parachutists behind our lines, particularly in the vicinity of our larger headquarters. These were
special groups of trained killers, who had been schooled to
get into our headquarters with the sole purpose of killing
Generals Eisenhower, Bradley, Patton and Hodges and
our higher Air Force Generals so as to spread confusion in
our ranks. These men all spoke perfect English and wore
American officers' uniforms and carried what looked like
authentic credentials. The sentries had been ordered to
shoot to kill anyone, even if he looked like an American
officer, who attempted to enter any of the higher headquarters.

The air was tense and we worked feverishly all day, the 20th, and well into the night. We were billeted at first in rooms scattered through the town and ate at the 12th Army Group mess. A tight curfew was clamped on the town and no one except officers on duty or returning to their quarters was allowed on the streets after dark. Half-tracks filled with armed soldiers, and armored cars, patrolled the streets all night, and as we went to our quarters from the headquarters late at night or in the early morning, walking along the silent streets, we would hear the rumble of a half-track in the distance, coming swiftly toward us. As it got near, flashlights would shine on us and we would be ordered to halt and show our credentials before being allowed to pass on.

During these first nights in Luxembourg we slept with our clothes on and our jeeps and drivers were always near at hand and ready to go. We did not unpack our baggage. The Germans were still driving desperately forward and the force of their offensive was by no means spent. All this time they continued to send in new divisions as reinforcements. General Patton was driving his forces head-on into them as they tried to advance, but the tide of battle flowed back and forth each day.

Every few minutes, all night long, the air raid sirens would howl and whine as German planes came over. The nights were made terrible by these screeching, mournful sounds, which sent civilians rushing to their air raid shelters. It was well-nigh impossible to get any sleep. After the second night, General Patton, who always did the sensible thing, ordered the sirens shut off entirely, so we could get some sleep. He figured it was better to have a few killed out of their shelters than to have everybody put out of their minds from the continual din and lack of sleep.

It was thrilling to go to the window when we heard the drone of the approaching planes and watch our antiaircraft guns send red tracer shells to pierce the sky. As these red shells laced the dark sky in search of enemy planes, you could hardly help thinking of the words of our National Anthem—"the rockets' red glare, the bombs bursting in air".

It was now only a few days before Christmas and momentous developments were taking place. Major Wolf, my executive officer, had returned from his search for VIII Corps Headquarters, which he found at Neufchateau. He also brought information that the 110th Regiment of the 28th Division was holding the town of Wiltz. The other two regiments of the division, the 109th and 112th, were out of contact. General Middleton, commander of the VIII Corps, had ordered the 101st Airborne Division, which had been in reserve in France, to close in the Bastogne area and to hold at all costs. The two regiments of the 106th Infantry Division were cut off and surrounded, but were still fighting and were being supplied by air. Eventually, however, all members of these regiments were killed or captured.

G-2 reported that the situation on V Corps (First Army) front was fluid and uncertain. More divisions of the Sixth Panzer Army were moving into the break-through area. The enemy penetrations by armor were being supported by infantry, and more parachutists and spies were being dropped behind our lines each night. The main enemy effort appeared to be south of Malmedy and the roads east of Trier continued to be clogged with traffic.

Scraps of information continued bad. The 101st Airborne Division, one combat command of the 9th Armored Division, and one combat command of the 10th Armored Division, and elements of the 28th Infantry Division all were reported completely surrounded in the Bastogne area. However, they had plenty of ammunition and supplies and were slugging it out with the enemy and not

trying to get out of the pocket. Brigadier General Mc-
Auliff, assistant division commander, was in command of
this Bastogne group since the division commander was in
the States on leave. In one day this fighting American
group knocked out 55 enemy tanks, by ground count.

The main enemy effort now was clearly toward
Bastogne. An increasing use of captured U. S. equipment
was noted. The enemy was using Sherman tanks and
American Army trucks with our white stars still on them.
They had not even taken time to have them painted out.
Many enemy agents and soldiers in U. S. uniforms were
picked up west of the Meuse River a hundred miles behind our lines. All bridges across the Meuse were being
mined by our service troops for possible future demolition,
and the bridges were under constant guard. Any persons
approaching them from either direction were screened.

Besides our Third Army Headquarters and 12th Army
Group Headquarters, there also were operating in Luxem-
bourg city the headquarters of the Ninth Air Force, the
XIX Tactical Air Force, our XII Corps and of three or
four divisions. Headquarters of III Corps was in Arlon,
Belgium, about 40 miles farther west.

In a news broadcast at this time, we heard that the
Nazi Ardennes offensive had caused a boom in the stock
market at home and that the market had reached a new
7-year high. This indicated to us that the people at
home figured that the German drive might be successful
and that the war might go on indefinitely.

A day or so after the group at Bastogne was cut off
completely and surrounded, the German General in command of the attacking force sent a message to General
McAuliff, telling him his troops were completely surrounded, that there was no hope for them, and demanding
that they surrender to save their lives.

General McAuliff sent back his famous and historic reply: "To the Commanding German General—NUTS!"

An interesting little side light on this message:—several of our French Liaison officers asked what our General meant when in his message he had replied "nuts!" They did not know how to translate it. We wondered what the Heinie general thought, when he got the message and tried to translate it.

And then occurred one of the most dramatic and important incidents of the whole war.

At the Third Army Staff briefing on the morning of 23 December the G-3 Air Officer, Lt. Colonel Pat Murray, made one of the finest speeches possible. He said that his weather report showed that there would be fair flying weather by 1000, and that the next day also should be clear.

Remember, at this point, that General Eisenhower had imposed a 48-hour news blackout for security reasons, and that the news at home from the fighting front was 48 hours behind events. This means that the great news about the break in the weather, which those at home heard on the radio Christmas morning, was known to General Patton's staff on that momentous morning of 23 December.

The weather did begin to clear on 23 December, the first time in weeks and sunrise on 24 December was the most beautiful any of us had ever seen, because it meant so much. Fresh-fallen snow sparkled, the air had turned frosty and it was an ideal day before Christmas, although we had little time to think of that.

Then our planes came, and that made the day perfect. Hundreds and hundreds, they laced the skies until the vapor trails formed a white mist almost as thick as the ground mist that had been keeping them earthbound for so long. It was beyond words; the most marvelous thing that could have happened.

At the Christmas Day briefing, the Air Officer, Colonel

Murray, announced: "It is prophesied by our weather men that the present clear weather will continue for at least another seven days."

That brought a general laugh from the staff, because there hadn't been that many clear days all winter and it just seemed impossible that such a miracle could continue. But the officer went on to explain that "through a freak of nature, two high-pressure areas from opposite directions had come together directly over us, that they were approximately of equal force, and that the clear weather would continue until one or the other weakened and gave way."

And that is what happened. Call it luck, a freak of nature, Providence, what you will, it was a thing that might not happen again at such a psychological moment for a hundred years. For seven days our air force blasted the Germans from the air, while our ground forces battered them on the ground.

The Bastogne pocket was still holding, and air drops with medical supplies, food and ammunition were made into the area almost daily. Then a large group of gliders was sent in and in them, besides much needed supplies, were nine doctors.

The enemy surrounding the Bastogne pocket was beginning to use white snow suits and his tanks were painted white. General Patton ordered our men in the front lines similarly equipped and the Belgian hills began to take on a ghostly appearance as the white figures flitted here and there. Even our artillery guns were painted white, which made them almost invisible in the fields and woods except when the red flashes would show up as they fired. And under the snow many bodies lay for days during this bitter fighting, covered only with the soft white blanket of nature.

Then, on 27 December, came big news! Combat Command Reserve of the 4th Armored Division, accompanied by elements of the 80th Infantry Division finally broke through to Bastogne, where the remnants of the beleaguered divisions still fought doggedly. Then we knew at last that the Battle of the Bulge would be an American victory and not a crushing defeat.

Forty trucks loaded with supplies and several ambulances which had been held in readiness for several days, were rushed through the first night. The road, however, had to be kept open by heavy fighting even after they passed through.

For some time after the contact with the troops in Bastogne was established, the Germans continued to attack both sides of the corridor desperately, but General Patton sent reinforcing columns up each side to widen it. Still it was several days before the contact was assured and all that time the town of Bastogne continued under threat.

Three of our corps, the VIII, III and XII now were attacking vigorously from the south while our XX Corps held on the east toward Germany. The situation still was exceedingly mobile. Brigadier General Edward T. Williams, Third Army Artillery Officer, ordered a number of our artillery groups attached directly to divisions for the attack, and many battalions, in turn, were attached to combat teams.

More than 1,700 tons of our ammunition had been captured by the Germans and 18 of our L-4 Cub artillery observation planes had either been captured or deliberately destroyed by our men to prevent capture, in the initial German advance. About 1 January, 20 ME-109's attacked our airfield at Metz, a long way behind our lines, and destroyed 20 of our planes on the ground, damaged 17 and killed a number of our men. The enemy planes came in to attack the field from all directions.

In one day there were 138 enemy air raids over the Third Army front and 361 enemy aircraft were knocked down.

Our 6th Armored Division reported that the fighting in the eastern sector of the Bastogne salient was the most severe in which it had engaged since it had been in France.

All this time the enemy continued to commit new divisions in the salient. On one day three new enemy divisions were identified, the 1st SS, the 3d Panzer and a Volksgrenadier division. Some of the new arrivals had been brought from Holland and some from Norway, and all were fresh and well-equipped.

Both the Germans and we were attacking at the same time and the battle raged to and fro. Our troops would attack and capture a town and several miles of territory. The next day the enemy would counterattack and retake the town and part of the ground. Then we would again take it from them. On one day alone there were 17 counterattacks against our Third Army troops.

During this period the enemy continually hurled 11-inch longrange shells from railroad guns into the city of Luxembourg. They also sent a new type of rocket into the town, particularly during the night. Several casualties occurred at headquarters buildings.

By the first week of January more than a third of the territory of the Ardennes salient had been recaptured from the enemy. The fighting continued bitter and the roads were icy or covered with snow and the temperature hovered near zero. Some days were clear, others were cloudy or overcast and again there would be more snow. It remained constantly bitter cold and our men suffered from the weather as well as the severe fighting. The only consolation was that the Germans were suffering more than we, for our men had warmer clothing and better food and we were slowly pushing them back. Our morale was high, for we were winning.

During the worst of the fighting at Christmas time, most of our men had been given a real turkey dinner. Not all got it on Christmas Day. Some got it just before and some a day or two after. Small groups were brought back a short distance from the fighting lines and, in so far as was humanly possible, were given hot turkey dinners with all the trimmings. The troops surrounded at Bastogne were not even contacted until 27 December, but as soon as possible after that they, too, were given their turkey dinner. It was deeply appreciated by the men, who felt that they had been remembered by those at home.

As late as 7 January our G-2 reported that one new enemy division had been identified in the salient. The most significant developments, however, were negative, he said—chiefly lack of aggressiveness on the part of the enemy. There were indications of some enemy withdrawals. There were reports that the enemy screening forces were made up of elements of many units to conceal identities and movements in the rear.

Our air reconnaissance also reported that much of the enemy's feverish activity in the rear areas, especially in the vicinity of Trier, had quieted down considerably.

The situation in the salient, however, was still fluid, and numerous and aggressive attacks still were being made against our troops as they pushed forward. Third Army artillery was more active than at any period since D-Day. Our III Corps, which had the heaviest artillery support of any corps, fired an average of 25,000 rounds daily, much of it to repel German counterattacks. In the pocket east of Bastogne, 5,500 tons of artillery ammunition was fired during one week.

By 13 January our G-2 reported that the German 9th Panzer Division in the west was covering an attempted withdrawal on our VIII Corps front, while in the pocket east of Bastogne the enemy 5th Paratroop Division was attempting to cover a withdrawal. The next day the 5th Paratroop Division was overrun by our troops and we reached the Houffalize-St. Vith road, one of their main supply roads. There was a steady stream of enemy traffic now on the roads going in a northeasterly direction. Our drive into the heart of the salient was being slowed down by enemy road blocks, demolitions and mine fields.

The enemy now was employing a unique replacement system. He was sending in complete small units to reinforce his shrinking larger units. Many times these reinforcing units were from other divisions.

By 17 January our 11th Armored Division (VIII Corps) in the west had contacted the 2d Armored Division of the VII Corps (First Army), which was pushing down from the north. The contact was made just south of Houffalize. By this contact, the one British corps, the XXX, which had been in the far western tip of the Bulge, was pinched out and returned to the British Second Army in the north.

Troops of our III Corps now were in the towns of Wiltz and Diekirch and had cut the St. Vith main highway.

On 23 January our XIX Tactical Air Force had one of its best days in the air, when 627 sorties were flown as the planes shuttled every minute during flying weather, dropping 263 tons of bombs in the front of Third Army along the Our River and in the Prum area. Our bombers had knocked out the bridge at Dasburg and enemy vehicles simply piled up near Eisenbach. While our ground forces pressed relentlessly against them and our artillery shelled them, the planes shuttled in and strafed and bombed. As they continued to pile up they were massacred. The slaughter was terrific.

In what was left of the Ardennes or Bastogne Bulge, the Germans were still resisting stubbornly on both the north and south flanks and attempting to withdraw in the center.

By 26 January both our III and XII Corps had reached and taken the high ground west of the Clerf River. There still was the equivalent of two enemy divisions west of the German border, but they were trying desperately to get behind the Siegfried Line. Our troops nicknamed this high ground the "Skyline Drive." From its heights you could clearly overlook the pillboxes, dragons' teeth and other defenses of the Siegfried Line.

Enemy movement continued toward the north and east and by 28 January our Third Army troops had reached the Luxembourg-German border in several places. At some points our troops now were two miles east of where von Rundstedt had started his power drive on 16 December, just a little more than a month before. The Battle of the Bulge was over.

This Ardennes Campaign was without doubt the most concentrated and the bloodiest operation of the Third Army during the whole war. All of the ground which the enemy had seized in his all-out attack was regained. Every inch of ground in the sweep in both directions was bitterly contested. Some of it was taken and retaken several times and all of the fighting had taken place in the coldest weather, with the temperature often at or near zero and the ground covered with snow and ice.

Third Army losses during this campaign were the heaviest of any of its operations. In the slightly less than six weeks we lost 4,796 killed, 22,109 wounded and 5,319 missing, a total of 32,224 casualties.

On the other hand, losses inflicted on the enemy by the Third Army alone were estimated at 32,000 killed and 88,600 wounded and we took 23,218 prisoners, a total of known and estimated enemy casualties of 143,818.

13

The Eifel Hills to the Rhine
Capture of Coblenz and Saar Basin

(28 January—21 March, 1945)

IN the seven weeks following the Ardennes victory, General Patton regrouped his forces and drove through the vaunted Siegfried Line, exerting continual pressure on all fronts. He drove his armored columns, supported by infantry, sometimes east, sometimes north, at other times south.

He used four corps in the beginning, the III, VIII, XII and XX. The III Corps had the 6th Cavalry Group, the 17th Airborne and the 6th Armored Division. The VIII Corps had the 4th, 87th and 90th Infantry and 11th Armored Divisions. The XII Corps had the 2d Cavalry Group, the 5th, 76th and 80th Infantry Divisions and the 4th Armored Division. The XX Corps at first was composed of the 3d Cavalry Group and the 26th and 94th Infantry Divisions and a little later the 10th Armored Division.

During the campaign the III Corps reverted to the First Army, but the 28th Infantry and 12th Armored Divisions were added to the Third Army and attached to its Corps.

In his many and varied drives General Patton confused and confounded the enemy. They never were sure where he was going to hit next nor how heavy the blow would be. They completely misjudged where his main effort was being exerted and built up their reserves and reinforce-

PATTON AND HIS THIRD ARMY

ments in the sector of one Corps, when suddenly he broke through in another sector, and it was then too late.

In this campaign, our columns drove through directly east more than sixty miles to the Rhine. Patton then pushed two Corps through this opening and, after they had reached various points to the east, he quickly regrouped his forces and suddenly turned the two Corps directly south. In this way he overran supply dumps and rear installations and then cut back toward the southwest and squeezed all of the German forces between the two jaws of a giant nutcracker and decimated or captured practically all of them.

General Patton had always said that the last great battle against the Germans would be fought west of the Rhine. He said that if the bulk of them could be killed or captured west of the Rhine, only isolated groups would be left to fight east of the river and the going would be comparatively easy. It worked out just as he had prophesied.

By 30 January, units of the Third Army had crossed the Our River and were inside Germany in two places. The town of Sinz, Germany, had been captured and we were again fighting in the Siegfried Line. There was house-to-house fighting in Sinz and other fortified towns in the line. Many of the forts were camouflaged as ordinary houses or farms. Actually they were built of heavy steel and concrete. The line had been built with typical German thoroughness and ingenuity. There was supporting fire from all pillboxes and forts.

On 6 February all four of our Corps attacked at dawn, preceded by a heavy artillery preparation. In crossing the various rivers on the way to Germany, our troops were greatly impeded by high water and swift currents and by barbed wire which the enemy had strung along the banks under the water.

Each of the hundreds of forts and pillboxes had to be

attacked individually and taken practically in hand-to-hand fighting. Many of the walls were from four to six feet thick, of steel and concrete, and the doors were of heavy steel, which could be blown only by bringing direct fire against them with bazookas or self-propelled guns.

Two days after the start of our four-corps attack, we had crossed the German frontier at ten places between Echternach and Clervaux. But German resistance was stubborn. Our troops first got across the rivers in assault boats, then cables were run across for foot bridges, and later treadway and Bailey bridges to carry trucks and armor were built. A great deal of this difficult bridging had to be done at night, under enemy fire and working in the cold and swollen streams. The enemy fought desperately in his defense of the river lines. All types of fire were used from the Siegfried fortifications—small arms, automatic weapons, artillery, nebelwerfer and mortar fire.

For a whole week our troops pushed forward slowly, enlarging our bridgeheads, clearing pillboxes and consolidating previous gains. By 11 February we had captured Prum and had entered Vianden. The enemy defended stubbornly and launched many small and medium counterattacks against us, but General Patton never let up his pressure. In one day 32 deserters from the 256th Volksgrenadier Division entered our lines bearing "safe conduct passes" which had been dropped on them by our planes or had been shot behind their lines by our artillery. This was encouraging, but unfortunately it was only an isolated instance.

On 11 February the III Corps passed to the First Army.

At this time our air reconnaissance reported columns of enemy vehicles moving in a southerly and southwesterly direction from Bitburg, apparently to reinforce their lines and to counter the thrust of our XII Corps. Tactical

Reconnaissance also reported heavy rail movements in the Kaiserslautern-Homburg and Trier-Wittlich areas and rail and road traffic in Germany east of the Rhine. All these movements were toward the west.

Now a new air force started operations. It was called the French Western Airforce and flew captured German planes. The French Army was trying hard to get back on its feet.

On 20 February the 10th Armored Division, which recently had been attached to the XX Corps, passed through the 94th Infantry Division and attacked. Instead of continuing to the east in the direction the 94th had been heading, it immediately turned north toward the ancient city of Trier, clearing up the territory in the triangle formed by the Moselle and the Saar Rivers as it went. The move took the Heinies completely by surprise and the first day the division advanced north more than eight miles and reached a point less than four miles from the junction of the two rivers.

The 2d Cavalry Group of XII Corps was moving south at the same time and it, together with elements of the 10th Armored Division, mopped up everything west of the Moselle. At the same time one combat command of the 10th Armored, with a regiment of the 94th Division attached, advanced and captured Saarburg.

G-2 reported that the high-light of enemy information was the complete disorganization of resistance in the Saar-Moselle triangle. All of the Third Army Corps were now attacking successfully.

In about three weeks since General Patton had launched his attack 29 January, the 6th Armored Division had destroyed 72 pillboxes; the 11th Armored, 171; the 90th Infantry, 391; the 4th Infantry, 223, and the 87th Infantry, 79, a total for the one Corps, the VIII, of 936 enemy pillboxes destroyed or captured. The other two corps had similar records. Mines, road blocks and terrain were becoming our chief obstacles as enemy resistance collapsed in the Saar-Moselle triangle against the 10th Armored and the 94th Infantry Divisions.

The weather had been spotty and frequently not good for flying during these days, but many jet-propelled enemy planes had been seen from time to time. On one day alone, 30 were observed. On 22 February the weather cleared after 1000 and our air had one of its greatest days in all history. Our XIX Tactical Air Force had a field day in Third Army front and in addition, Ninth Bomber Command had 445 bombers over targets in Germany. Seven hundred seventy bombers escorted by fighters came up from Italy and attacked targets in southern Germany, and the Royal Air Force also had a field day.

All this time General Patton's ground forces exerted pressure relentlessly all along Third Army front. The fighting was stiff and bitter as the Siegfried Line crumbled before the blows, but he never let up the pressure for an instant. Each day, and frequently at night, he was out, as were the members of his staff, visiting front line units, getting the latest information and giving encouragement. The Old Man was always an inspiration, and he was always there if an especially difficult assault—crossing of a river was being made, or if the combat engineers were having a hard time erecting a bridge under fire.

It was at one of these crossings, over the Sauer River, that General Patton waded out into the icy water up to his knees and a newspaper correspondent sent in a dispatch that the General had swum the river at the head of his troops.

In the XX Corps zone, as it approached the crossing of the Saar right in the heart of the Siegfried defenses, the 5th Ranger Battalion was attached to the 94th Infantry

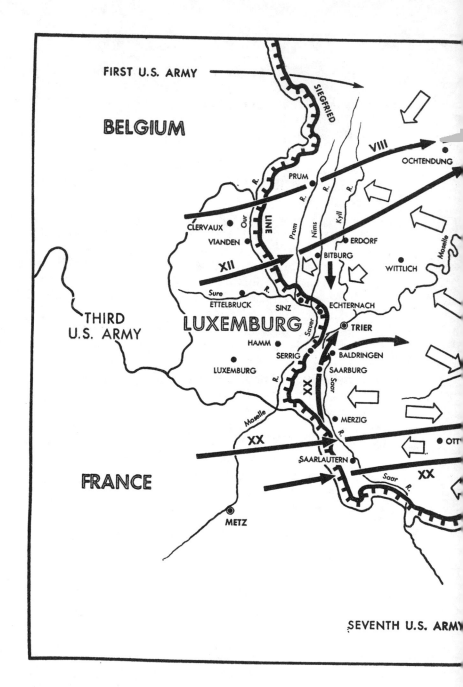

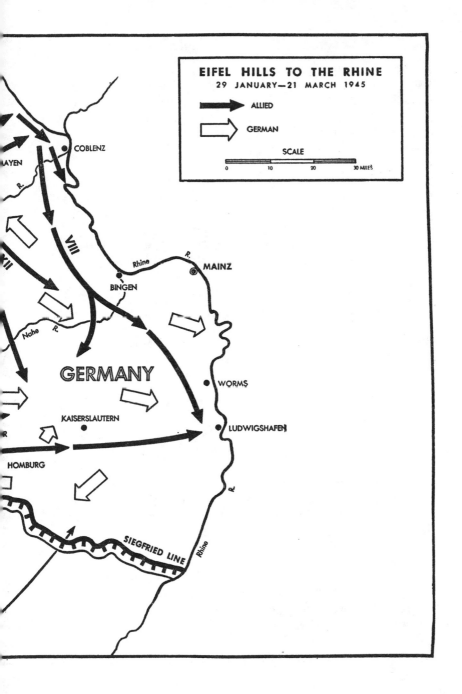

EIFEL HILLS TO THE RHINE
29 JANUARY—21 MARCH 1945

ALLIED
GERMAN

SCALE
0   10   20   30 MILES

COBLENZ

AYEN

VIII

Rhine

R.

MAINZ

BINGEN

Nahe   R.

GERMANY

WORMS

KAISERSLAUTERN

LUDWIGSHAFEN

HOMBURG

SIEGFRIED LINE

Rhine

R.

Division. With the greatest difficulty, Serrig, on the east bank of the river, was finally cleared and the bridgehead expanded. Our troops advanced two miles and seized high ground, cutting the main road east of Saarburg. A treadway bridge was completed and many supporting weapons were moved across—antitank guns, light and medium tanks, half-tracks and self-propelled guns.

General Patton ordered continual pressure exerted and stiff probing into enemy defenses. In some sections the enemy appeared confused by the speed of our attack. In other places, as in the area opposite Hamm, the 5th Ranger Battalion met stubborn resistance. East of Saarlautern there was heavy fighting. In one section a new Volksgrenadier division was identified. Prisoners reported that it had only been mobilized on 14 February. The troops were armed only with carbines and their morale was low. The Krauts were scraping the bottom of their manpower barrel, but were doing everything possible to hold us where their best defenses were located.

On 26 February, in XII Corps zone, the 4th Armored Division broke loose with the 80th Division following closely, and advanced five miles, seizing bridges intact over the Prum and Nims rivers. Next day the 4th Armored advanced another nine miles to the high ground overlooking Erdorf, on the Kyll River. The 80th Infantry, mopping up behind, made six miles the same day. In the rapid advance of the 4th Armored, it bypassed several towns from which the enemy opened fire on the flanks and rear of the division after it had passed. The 5th Infantry Division at the same time advanced four miles, capturing a bridge intact.

While the XII Corps was pushing rapidly to the east, the 10th Armored Division of XX Corps advanced another five miles to the north and captured Zerf just south of Trier.

Our G-2 now reported heavy counterattacks of infantry and assault guns against the divisions of the XX Corps. The 11th Panzer Division was identified in this sector, also the 2d and 6th SS Mountain Divisions and units made up of troops from the Noncommissioned Officers' School at Heidelberg. Another identification was the 262d Infantry Division from the Russian front. This was the first division contacted which had been brought from the eastern to the western front.

The enemy had evidently again been fooled by General Patton's tactics and had wrongly estimated that our main attack was coming in the XX Corps zone, instead of farther north in the zone of the XII Corps.

The 10th Armored continued to advance to the north, gaining four miles and capturing Baldringen. It was now about six miles directly south of Trier. Our troops were encountering strongly defended road blocks, some of which were mined; also extensive mine fields covered by small arms, antitank guns and bazookas.

In the north our troops had crossed the Prum River and entered Bitburg. There were numerous counterattacks, but on one day alone 7,000 prisoners were taken, bringing our total so far in this operation above 40,000.

On 1 March Supreme Allied Headquarters warned the citizens of Trier by radio to evacuate the city, as it was about to receive a heavy bombardment. This it did, from the air and from our artillery. The following day the 10th Armored Division broke through, captured a bridge intact and took the city. At the same time the 76th Division of XII Corps was approaching the city from the north and was only three and a half miles away. All along the Moselle River our troops met heavy machine-gun fire and fire from antiaircraft guns used as field artillery.

All the area between Saarburg and Trier was cleared but the 10th Armored met stiff fighting through the city of Trier from Volksturm troops as well as the Wehrmacht. More than 3,000 prisoners were rounded up in the town. Elements of the 10th Armored advanced northeast of the city, endeavoring to take a bridge intact across the Kyll River, but they found it blown. They made contact, however, with the 76th Infantry Division of the XII Corps about two miles north of Trier.

All during this period our air reported increased enemy air activity, particularly jet-propelled planes.

The day after the capture of Trier, I visited the 10th Armored Division and had lunch in a former German barracks with Major General Wm. H. H. Morris, Jr., the division commander, and some of his staff. An occasional enemy shell was falling in the town and many of the dead had not yet been removed. There were also a number of snipers still in the town. One of the lieutenants from Third Army Headquarters and his jeep driver were killed that day while visiting the city.

Trier itself was a shambles. The air and our artillery had almost completely wrecked the place. I thought again of what the German prisoner had cynically said when he quoted what he called the only true statement Hitler had ever made: "Give me Germany for ten years and at the end of that time no one will be able to recognize it". Practically all the buildings had been wrecked or damaged. The streets were cluttered with rubble except where our bulldozers had cleared some of the main ones so our troops could pass through.

Trier was one of the oldest cities on the European continent and was formerly a Roman town. Its early name was Treves and it was a famous resort. Some of the old Roman baths had been preserved and the famous old ruin of the Porta Nigra was a familiar landmark to sightseers before the war. Ironically enough, this ancient ruin was untouched by the bombing and shelling, but the well-known Porta Nigra Hotel across the street was ruined. The front wall still stood and one could enter through the door, but most of the hotel was demolished.

The pre-war population of Trier had been about 80,000 and it had been one of the railroad centers and bases from which von Rundstedt had launched his Ardennes offensive the previous December, but now scarcely more than a thousand civilians were left. A few miserable creatures here and there peered furtively at us from the wrecks of buildings or from cellars. A few even attempted to smile at us, but most had only lifeless, vacant stares. Household goods, clothes, books, furniture, silverware, pictures and such things were strewn about everywhere. The inhabitants evidently had evacuated in a hurry on General Eisenhower's warning and many of the buildings had been rifled by civilians and troops. At one place we found, all over the ground, hundreds of pieces of German paper money, among them many 20,000-mark notes.

At lunch that day General Morris told a story about one of his units. He had been asked how many prisoners his division was taking. He said that a week or two before, at the start of their drive for Trier, a lieutenant colonel commanding one of his battalions had been severely wounded. He had been placed on a stretcher and two medical corpsmen started to carry him to the rear, when the Heinies counterattacked. As they approached, they shot the two litter bearers, and then as they neared the wounded officer lying on the stretcher on the ground, they saw that he was alive, so they shot him too. Other men of the battalion saw it all, and General Morris said that from then on that battalion had refused to take any prisoners. One could hardly blame them.

By this time the Germans were well reinforced and built up opposite the XX Corps, on the south of Third Army front. It was there they figured General Patton was making his main effort and they were prepared for it.

Then, like lightning, General Patton struck in the north, first with his XII Corps and then with his VIII. The 4th Armored Division, still commanded by the intrepid leader Major General Hugh Gaffey, who had been its commander when it made its historic breakthrough in December to the relief of Bastogne, was assembled at Bitburg. On the morning of 5 March it attacked with great dash toward the east, through the 5th Infantry Division's Kyll River bridgehead. With one regiment of the 5th Infantry motorized to accompany it, it gained on the first day from four to fifteen miles and captured a bridge intact.

On the same day, the VIII Corps also attacked. The 90th Infantry Division passed through the 6th Armored Division and gained four and a half miles and the 11th Armored advanced four to six miles. The 87th Division had finished clearing 113 pillboxes and, without a rest, it and all the other infantry divisions continued the attack, moving steadily forward to the east. By 7 March the 11th Armored had advanced another seventeen miles and captured the Commanding General of the German XV Corps and his entire staff.

The Heinies now were diligently digging in along all river banks for the defense. The Eifel hills, with their steep slopes and many rivers, were ideal for defense. Numerous defended tank ditches were encountered and many counterattacks were made against our troops as new enemy divisions were brought against us in an effort to halt the drive.

The 17th SS Panzer and the 6th SS Mountain Divisions were identified among these reinforcements. But General Patton's armored spearheads had advanced thirty-five miles in two days and were now within twenty miles of the Rhine.

The pressure now was stepped up to give the enemy

no time to dig in or reinforce. The following day the 4th Armored, with one regiment of the 5th Infantry motorized and attached (both of the XII Corps) advanced another 18 to 19 miles, bypassing the town of Mayen, and reached high ground overlooking the Rhine just north of Coblenz. Our Third Army spearheads had reached the Rhine after pushing forward 55 miles from the Kyll River in 58 hours.

Next day the 11th Armored Division of VIII Corps, with a regiment of the 90th Infantry Division attached, advanced 22 miles east and made contact with elements of the 4th Armored, in the vicinity of Ochtendung. They met stiff enemy resistance at first, as the Germans were well entrenched. They broke through this defense line and again met strong opposition four miles farther east, but after breaking through this they advanced against only scattered resistance. In this drive large numbers of prisoners were taken; a whole field hospital was overrun and much artillery and other equipment was captured. By 10 March the 11th Armored had reached the Rhine and captured several towns along the river. In its dash, it also captured a German Major General commanding the 277th Volksgrenadier Division and his whole staff.

A glance at the map shows that the Moselle River runs northeast from Trier to join the Rhine at Coblenz. Both our XII and VIII Corps, spearheaded by the 4th and 11th Armored Divisions, had reached the Rhine in the area north of the Moselle. Many of the enemy had surrendered as our troops advanced, but a considerable number had withdrawn south of the Moselle. Our men, including of course the infantry divisions of both corps, now mopped up all this area north of the Moselle and west of the Rhine. The enemy still tried to hold bridgeheads north of the Moselle for a few days and occasional small arms fire and sporadic artillery fire came from the east side of the Rhine.

Tactical reconnaissance reported much rail movement, mostly east of the Rhine. Our air forces, in this day or two, lost several aircraft under mysterious circumstances. Wings fell off as the planes flew and the bodies exploded and disintegrated in the air. To the best of my knowledge, no cause for these tragedies was ever discovered.

After a day or two of mopping up north of the Moselle and some slight regrouping of his forces, General Patton was now ready to spring the trap which would bring the remaining German troops, numbering more than 100,000, within the jaws of his giant nutcracker. These enemy troops, remnants of the German First and Seventh Armies, were south of the Moselle and west of the Rhine, in a region known as the Palatinate.

On 13 March the XII Corps attacked south, using the 5th and 90th Infantry Divisions to cross the Moselle and establish bridgeheads. The 11th Armored Division of VIII Corps was attached to XII Corps, and the cavalry units and 76th, 87th and 89th Infantry Division of VIII Corps relieved the two armored divisions in their mopping up operations, so that the armor could be ready to attack south as soon as the bridgeheads had been established.

The missions of the three Corps for this operation were as follows: XII Corps to attack across the Moselle and drive south; VIII Corps, after completing the mopping up north of the Moselle, to capture Coblenz and then to follow the XII Corps south, clearing everything along the Rhine; XX Corps to attack and drive to the east. It was still along the Saar River, 80 miles west of the Rhine.

In the early morning of 15 March all three Corps were on the move. The Third Army had been given two additional divisions for this operation—the 28th Infantry to the VIII Corps for the capture of Coblenz, and the 12th

Armored to XX Corps to drive east with the 10th Armored, after passing through the infantry divisions. The VIII Corps captured Coblenz quickly after a lightning attack and then pushed south along the west bank of the Rhine. On 17 March, the XII Corps—the 4th Armored with regiments of the 5th and 90th Infantry Divisions—broke loose and advanced from 20 to 30 miles to the Nahe River, south of Bingen on the Rhine. The 11th Armored also made wide gains. The breakthrough gained momentum against badly disorganized enemy resistance, as our armored columns now were in the rear of all the forces facing the XX Corps farther west, and were playing havoc with their supply installations. Many road blocks, some defended, others not, were overrun.

Our air reported seeing large bodies of troops marching along the roads in the rear areas. When they were attacked they waved white flags.

The XX Corps, driving east, at first met stubborn resistance, which later became disorganized. The air, in XX Corps zone, reported enemy vehicular movement toward the east and prisoners' statements indicated a possible withdrawal. But now it was too late, for General Patton had them in a vise.

The 10th Armored reported that difficult terrain and stubbornly defended road blocks were the principal obstacles, although bazooka-carrying infantry also were attacking the armored columns. The 94th Infantry Division reported that enemy resistance centered on towns and road junctions. There were many counterattacks by small groups and many road blocks were defended by dug-in infantry and self-propelled guns. In some sectors the enemy still defended bitterly from pillboxes, trenches and dug-in strong points, which frequently were mined and booby-trapped.

Gradually all enemy resistance was becoming disorganized, as many made desperate efforts to escape.

Each day our advances continued and on 19 March all four armored divisions—the 4th, 10th, 11th and 12th—were making big gains and our infantry divisions were following them closely, mopping up as they went. Some of the Third Army's most spectacular advances were made on this day.

Our momentum was accelerating from day to day. The 10th Armored went 15 miles and cut the Homburg-Kaiserslautern highway. The 12th Armored, after a 15-mile advance, was astride the railroad at the junction of the Kaiserslautern-Worms branches. The 11th Armored moved up 15 miles and made contact with the 12th Armored. The 4th Armored pushed forward several miles and cut the Worms-Bingen highway about twelve miles southwest of Mainz.

Resistance disintegrated rapidly as our infantry and armored spearheads drove farther into and behind the enemy lines, overrunning rear installations and supply dumps. Much equipment and large numbers of prisoners were captured. Difficult terrain slowed our progress somewhat and here and there, as in the vicinity of Ottweiler, some of the enemy fought desperately to keep open the narrow escape gap to the east. There was one strong counterattack by SS troops near Ottweiler and bitter house-to-house fighting in Ottweiler itself, where many mines were found. Attention of all units was again called to the danger of time bombs and booby traps.

By 21 March our columns had captured Worms, population 50,661; Mainz, 158,533; Ludwigshaven, 144,425; Kaiserslautern, 70,713; and Coblenz, 65,251, and had cleared all the west bank of the Rhine. Enemy forces could be seen feverishly building defenses on the east bank of the river, and they were dispersed by artillery fire.

The Third Army now had linked up with the Seventh Army pushing up from the southwest and together they decimated the German First and Seventh Armies.

In addition to capturing 2,934 square miles of territory, including the whole industrially great Saar Basin, the Third Army had taken more than 81,000 prisoners in this campaign, and had inflicted on the enemy casualties estimated at 7,700 killed and 14,600 wounded, a total of 103,300 put out of action.

General Patton's Third Army now stood along the west bank of the Rhine River, historic barrier behind which lay the heart of Hitler's Reich.

14

Forcing the Rhine and Across Germany—Entering Czechoslovakia and Austria

(22 March-8 May 1945)

O N 22 March, the Third Army held 100 miles along the west bank of the Rhine, although many pockets of enemy troops were being mopped up farther west of the river.

Our air reconnaissance reported increased enemy activity on the east bank of the river, where he continued to improve his defenses. Increased rail activity also was noted east of the Rhine, where numerous flat cars were observed loaded with motor transport and tanks. Marshaling yards, too, showed increased activity. Our infantry patrols crossing the river at night reported the enemy alert and sensitive.

General Patton realized there was no time to lose. The longer we waited to cross, the more time the enemy would have to build up and concentrate his forces behind this formidable river barrier and consequently the more casualties we would have when we finally did attempt to cross. He did not want to see a repetition of the situation of the previous September, when we had found the Siegfried Line defenses practically unmanned, but had had to draw back for lack of supplies, and then had found heavy and bloody going to get through later because the Germans had made good use of the time and had built up his forces.

General Patton had been considering improvising an air drop of his own, composed entirely of his own troops and planes, to take the enemy by surprise, before he could get thoroughly organized for defense of the river line. For this proposed drop he was considering using the small L-4 observation planes assembled from all the artillery battalions in the Army, numbering several hundred, plus the 32 L-5 liaison planes attached to our Army Headquarters. Each of these planes could carry only one passenger besides the pilot, but with several hundred of them, each carrying one infantryman, and making several trips an hour, it would not have taken long to transport several regiments over the river and behind the enemy fortifications. The little observation planes could land in any more or less level field, and in very small ones, at that. Our XIX Tactical Air Force could, of course, have provided air cover for the drop.

When General Patton learned, however, that up to that moment the enemy had not had time to build up in force across the river, and that the opposition would be comparatively light, especially if he moved across at once, he abandoned the plan for the air drop.

Great care and preparation had been made for a crossing by assault boats and bridges. For some time prior to the actual crossing, bridge building equipment had had first priority with the Third Army Quartermaster truck companies. They had been bringing this equipment up over long distances and depositing it under camouflage in strategic locations. The same trucks then returned for more equipment, taking with them on the trip west full loads of Nazi prisoners. Vast amounts of pontons, Baileys and treadway materials were hauled to the river in addition to assault boats and other amphibious landing craft. The latter were supplied and operated by the Navy.

The Rhine had long been thought a great barrier which would delay us and cause many casualties. Actually, so carefully had the preparations been made and so fast did General Patton move, that the crossing was a complete tactical surprise, not only to the Germans but to the whole world. There was no air or artillery preparation, in order that the enemy should have no advance notice of where the crossing was to be made.

On the night of 22-23 March, the 5th Infantry Division (XII Corps), supported by amphibious tanks, crossed the Rhine at Oppenheim, about ten miles south of Mainz, in the valley leading toward Frankfurt. It was an assault crossing with assault boats. The First Army already had crossed the river farther north, but that was across the Remagen railroad bridge, which had been captured intact. Ours was the first assault crossing and it was made quickly and easily. By noon of the first day, 23 March, the entire 5th Infantry Division was across with its attached antitank weapons, tank destroyers and some tanks. The bridgehead was quickly expanded to seven miles in width by six miles in depth. Then followed immediately the 90th Infantry Division and the 4th Armored.

Within 36 hours of the initial crossing, a treadway and a ponton bridge had been erected, and by the 24th both the 26th Infantry and the 6th Armored Divisions had crossed into the bridgehead area.

When the Germans realized what was taking place, they reacted violently, especially in the air. Great air activity developed in the bridgehead area and against the bridges themselves, where there was heavy bombing and strafing. The enemy made 115 air raids in one day in which 231 planes took part.

In the advance to the east after crossing the river, our troops encountered only sporadic resistance from small enemy groups. The initial surprise was so great that the first wave met no resistance and passed beyond sleeping enemy troops, who later were mopped up by succeeding waves.

There were a few counterattacks when the Germans realized what was taking place, but they were comparatively small and were quickly brushed aside by our on-rushing columns. The 4th Armored, with one regiment of the 26th Infantry attached, passed through the 5th and 90th Infantry Divisions and drove twenty miles, bypassing Darmstadt. The 90th Infantry, following, attacked and cleared that town.

By 26 March all units of XII Corps were well beyond the Rhine. The 6th Armored captured a damaged bridge across the Main River at Frankfurt and, followed by the 5th Infantry Division, was well into the industrial heart of the city. At first they met small arms and automatic weapons fire and high-velocity 88-mm fire. Later scattered resistance was encountered from police, firemen, air raid wardens and a few troops. The 5th Infantry Division finally cleared the city on 29 March.

A few days after our bridges were erected across the Rhine, our troops captured two enemy swimmers just above the bridge sites. They wore all-rubber heated suits with large rubber fins on their feet. They were equipped with explosives which could be floated, in watertight containers, just under the surface of the water. The swimmers were also equipped with tubes and breathing apparatus so they could get air while swimming under water. Their mission, of course, had been to blow our bridges.

In its zone of advance, the 4th Armored reported only scattered resistance, chiefly from towns. In most of the towns there was much opposition from police and civilians armed with small arms. Several new enemy divisions were being identified, but they were chiefly Volks-grenadier ones. At this time we recorded a new all-time record for one day's "take" of prisoners, with 18,800.

While the XII Corps was advancing thus, on 24 March the VIII Corps, composed of the 76th, 87th and 89th

Infantry Divisions, launched an attack by the 87th to cross the Rhine near Boppard. This crossing, also, was made in assault boats. It was met by heavy enemy resistance, as the Germans had continued to improve their defense positions on the east bank in that sector. Scattered small arms, machineguns, mortar and light artillery fire was sustained, but the crossing was successful. Then, on the next day, another bridgehead was secured at St. Goar by the 89th Infantry Division. Fire support for both these crossings was supplied by the 76th Infantry, from the west bank of the river, which followed over after the other two divisions were across.

On the night of 27-28 March, the XX Corps, composed of the 65th, 80th Infantry and 11th Armored Divisions, crossed both the Rhine and the Main Rivers in the vicinity of Mainz, just north of St. Goar. At first the resistance was stubborn and several counterattacks were made by infantry, with mortar fire and moderate artillery support, but no enemy air or armor was reported.

Almost all elements of Patton's Third Army now were across and in general the going was becoming easier. However, there was continued sporadic fighting. In Darmstadt our troops were fired on by civilians without even Volksturm bands on the arms, and orders were issued immediately that all armed civilians would be summarily shot.

The 5th Infantry Division reported house-to-house fighting in the large industrial center of Frankfurt. Intense mortar and artillery fire fell in the vicinity of our bridge site across the Main River and sporadic small arms fire was felt along the south bank of the Main east of Frankfurt. Street fighting was reported in Hanau and there were two counterattacks against the 4th Armored Division.

During the third week of April, the Third and First Armies made contact on the Elbe River and then, instead of continuing east toward Berlin, the Third Army was ordered to turn south-southeast. General Patton headed in the direction of Nurnberg to cut off the Southern Redoubt near Berchtesgaden, where the Nazis were expected to make their last stand.

American columns of armor and motor vehicles were burning up the roads of Germany. Hitler's wonderful four-lane, banked and graded autobahns were a delight to our boys, used to "stepping on the gas" on our roads back home. Hitler had built these roads, largely with borrowed funds, so he could rush troops from the center of Germany, he said, to any border of the Fatherland against the enemies who, according to Der Fuehrer, threatened Germany from every side. Actually they were built so that German troops could be rushed to every border to attack their neighbors. But now they proved a boomerang, for our columns roared along them right into the heart of Germany.

The armored columns could, of course, take care of themselves as they rushed eastward, but small groups of the enemy and individual snipers would attack single vehicles and small groups of vehicles in towns or traveling through woods, so for a time it was necessary to put all convoys under armored car protection.

Our Quartermaster truck companies had been doing an outstanding job all through France, Luxembourg and Belgium, but now in Germany, where the distances were even greater, they outdid their own records, moving troops, bringing up supplies of all kinds and hauling thousands of prisoners to the rear. As General Patton said: "The 2½-ton truck is our most valuable weapon."

With our air forces ranging all over enemy territory and our motor vehicles burning up the roads of Germany, we were truly an army on wings and wheels. German civilians looked on with utter amazement. Most of them seemed dull and stupid, and utterly dazed and disillusioned.

As was General Patton's method, he sometimes sent his armor ahead, followed by the infantry, and at other times he sent his infantry ahead, as in making a river crossing and forming a bridgehead, or in the storming of a city or a strong point. He employed his combined forces superbly, using first one and then another. He has been called our greatest tank expert, and so he was, but actually he was an expert with all arms of the service. He always used the right one at the right time and place. His infantry would make the opening, and after the hole in the enemy line had been made, he would send his armor dashing through to raise havoc with the enemy in the rear areas. At other times he would send his armored columns through first to smash the resistance and by-pass strong points, and then the infantry would follow to reduce the strong points and mop up all resistance.

On 28 March, while the Third Army was still driving east, General Patton ordered a reshuffling of his forces to provide the most effective fighting strength in all groups. The 11th Armored Division passed from XX Corps to XII Corps, and the 5th Infantry and 6th Armored Divisions passed from XII to XX Corps.

The 6th Armored drove rapidly northeast almost to Kassel. This drive of more than a hundred miles in three days was one of the fastest in the entire history of the Third Army. The 65th and 80th Infantry Divisions followed to mop up. There was little organized enemy resistance on the various fronts except at Kassel, where our forces were held up three days in reducing the city.

At this same time the 80th Infantry Division cleared Weisbaden. Resistance was disorganized on the whole, with ineffective delaying actions in towns and at critical terrain features, and only a few groups offered determined resistance. It was considered significant that the prisoners captured were from miscellaneous units.

Tactical reconnaissance reported considerable vehicular traffic behind enemy lines during these days—mixed motor transport, half-tracks, tanks and horse-drawn vehicles. A large amount of rail movement also was noted. One day 19 trains were observed, 17 of them moving west and southwest, all loaded with motor transport and armor. This indicated at least another division moving into the Third Army zone.

Civilians were caught laying mines at night in areas occupied by our troops. Two vehicles of Third Army Headquarters were lost near the town of Germscheid as a result of mines.

At the beginning of April, Third Army was advancing deep into Germany, with the XX Corps on the north and the XII on the south and the VIII Corps mopping up in the rear. On 3 April the VIII Corps was moved up and given a central zone between the XX and XII Corps, and the 4th Armored Division, which was already in this sector, passed under its control. The XII Corps now had the 11th Armored followed by the 26th and 90th Infantry Divisions, with the 71st Infantry Division mopping up in its rear. It was attacking east, but on 5 April General Patton ordered it to turn and attack south-southeast.

Spearheaded by the 11th Armored, the infantry divisions rotated, taking turns at following the armor closely, guarding the flanks and mopping up in the rear. The cities of Coburg, Neustadt and Bayreuth were cleared. A restraining line again had been placed on the Third Army at the Czechoslovak border and on 16 April the 90th Infantry Division reached it.

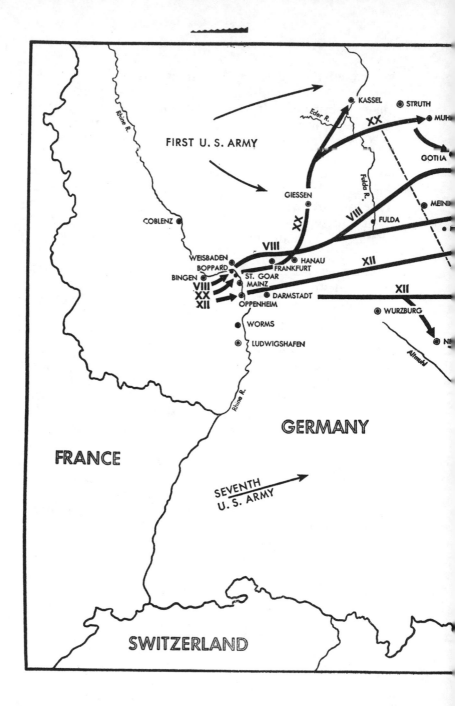

KASSEL ● STRUTH ●

MUH●

Eder R.

XX

GOTHA

Rhine R.

FIRST U. S. ARMY

Fulda R.

GIESSEN ●

MEINI●

COBLENZ ●

XX

VIII

FULDA ●

●

VIII

WEISBADEN ●

BOPPARD ●

HANAU ●

FRANKFURT ●

XII

BINGEN ●

ST. GOAR

MAINZ ●

VIII

XX

XII

OPPENHEIM

DARMSTADT ●

XII

WURZBURG ●

WORMS ●

N●

LUDWIGSHAFEN ●

Altmuhl

GERMANY

Rhine R.

FRANCE

SEVENTH
U. S. ARMY

SWITZERLAND

LEIPZIG

Saale R.

EN

RY WEIMAR ZEITZ

Mulde R.

DRESDEN

BUCHENWALD
CAMP

JENA

CHEMNITZ

VIII

OLDHAUSEN

COBURG

V

BAYREUTH

TIRSCHENREUTH

WEIDEN

PILSEN

CZECHOSLOVAKIA

DT

NURNBERG

NEUMARKT

HOHENFELD

XII

XX

REGENSBURG

Danube R.

III

XX

LANDAU

Danube

MOOSBURG

Isar R.

Inn R.

R.

LINZ

MUNICH

SALZBURG

BERCHTESGADEN

AUSTRIA

ACROSS THE RHINE TO VICTORY
22 MARCH—8 MAY 1945

ALLIED

SCALE

0   10   20   30   40   50   60   70
MILES

Meantime the VIII and XX Corps were still driving toward the east. The Third Army had joined up with the First Army at Giessen and the two armies had closed a pocket of 2,000 square miles between Frankfurt and Giessen. SS units continued to make strong stands, otherwise demoralized and disorganized enemy groups offered only token resistance before surrendering.

Many P. W.'s and much equipment were captured. Numerous enemy groups, cut off to the west, attempted to infiltrate through our lines and were made prisoners. Tanks of Third Army were running completely wild against light enemy opposition and had almost reached one of the main autobahns to Berlin. German traffic was becoming hopelessly tangled, but bypassed enemy troops and civilians continued to harass single or small groups of our vehicles along the roads.

Reports came from prisoners that the Germans were preparing poisoned sugar, coffee substitute, cigarettes and chocolate for our troops.

One day our air bombed a loaded German train. One plane swooped low to release its bomb. The train was loaded with ammunition and the resulting explosion not only destroyed the train but blew the plane and its crew to bits.

As our spearheads reached the Eder and Fulda river lines, enemy resistance stiffened. Stubborn opposition together with information from captured enemy documents and from prisoners indicated an enemy defense line in this area from Kassel southward. The XX Corps reported enemy opposition the strongest since it had crossed the Rhine. Bridges were blown at Heimboldhausen and the approaches to bridges were defended vigorously by bazooka teams, supported by tanks and assault guns. Our columns attacked strongly, however, and shortly the 6th Armored Division had crossed the

Fulda on a treadway bridge and a captured railroad bridge, and continued the drive east. The enemy defended from dug-in positions on commanding ground, and roads and defiles were covered by small arms and antitank fire. Overpasses and underpasses on the autobahns were blown and numerous ambush attacks were made against supply trains and vehicular convoys.

During the first week of April the 6th Armored Division captured Muhlhausen and the 80th Infantry Division finally took Kassel after house-to-house fighting. Several new enemy divisions began to appear in Third Army zone. A new division plus miscellaneous regiments on the south flank indicated a buildup there, while on the north flank the enemy defense stiffened and three counterattacks were repulsed. On 8 April a strong counterattack was made on the north flank and the town of Struth was retaken by the enemy. After heavy fighting, half of the enemy force of more than a thousand were killed or captured, nine tanks destroyed and Struth was back in our hands.

The 4th Armored (XX Corps) now passed through the 80th Infantry Division and drove east 35 miles in one day. One column passed three miles south of Jena, which fell, and just west of Weimar. At Weimar, seat of the ill-fated German republic which followed World War I, had been located a large German headquarters and near there also was the infamous Buchenwald concentration camp, which was liberated. Although the concentration camp was located only about a mile and a half from Weimer, every citizen of the town of 25,000 denied that he knew what had been taking place there. General Patton, therefore, ordered every citizen of the town, over seven, to be marched thru the camp under guard to behold the gruesome sights and to see firsthand the attrocities which had been committed by their countrymen. The

80th Division reached Erfurt and captured it after bitter fighting, and the 6th Armored passed through the 76th Infantry Division and advanced 40 miles to the Salle River.

There was no effective resistance to the rapid advance of our armored spearheads now, but there was stubborn fighting in key towns, with many counterattacks and increased sniper activity.

On 14 April the 4th Armored advanced 40 miles and seized the bridges over the Mulde River before they could be blown. The 80th Infantry cleared Jena. Zeitz was captured and 271 German guns were overrun in the town.

General Patton's armored columns had bypassed Leipzig and had reached a point only 40 miles from Dresden. Our whole XX Corps was now east of the Mulde River and our ground troops reported seeing Russian aircraft.

The garrison at Bayreuth stubbornly refused to surrender but was softened up by a joint application of air bombing and artillery concentrations and the town was then cleared.

Enemy vehicular traffic now began to show a trend toward the east and south. General Patton's Third Army had virtually cut the Reich in two, severing the main supply lines leading from Prussia to Saxony and to the mountains of Bavaria in the south.

On 17 April the restraining line was lifted, but Third Army troops were not yet allowed to drive into Czechoslovakia.

General Patton regrouped his forces once more and again attacked to the southeast and by 21 April the XII Corps had driven south as far as Weiden along the Czech border toward Austria. By the same day the 4th Armored (VIII Corps) cleared Gotha and the 65th Infantry Division took Neumarket, while the 80th Infantry Division entered Nurnberg. The 90th Infantry Division, mopping up behind the 4th Armored, captured more than

100 tons of gold bullion and priceless art objects in an unguarded salt mine near Gotha.

Vehicular traffic behind enemy lines became very active, with the trend definitely south. Much rail activity likewise was reported, also principally to the south. The Nazis were making a last desperate effort to reach their Southern Redoubt near Berchtesgaden, which our G-2 Intelligence had persistently reported well stocked with arms, ammunition, and other supplies.

Enemy air forces were still active, but our own air continually whittled them down. Daily our planes also destroyed enemy motor transport, armored vehicles, locomotives, railroad cars, horse-drawn vehicles and buildings and attacked air fields and railroad marshalling yards and cut rail lines. It was a repetition of the dash across France the preceding summer, and wrecked German vehicles and equipment were strewn along roads and through the fields.

The German Military Commission in the town of Chemnitz refused to surrender, so it was blasted by artillery and bombing.

The prisoner round-up mounted steadily from day to day. Now we took more than 25,000 in one day and a few days later more than 30,000. No one had time to bother about "capturing" them any more. When there were not enough trucks to carry them, they were just waved on down the roads to the west, toward France.

Disorganized enemy troops, as well as road blocks and other obstacles were swept aside or bypassed, as our drive southward gained momentum and our columns crossed the Naab River at several points over bridges captured intact. At Tirschenreuth the 90th Infantry Division captured 1,500 Hungarian troops, including two generals and four colonels, after only token resistance. At Hohenfeld 2,300 American and British prisoners, many of them airmen, were freed.

The last days of this campaign were distinguished by the wholesale rout of the enemy. General Patton's orders now were to strike to the south and seize Salzburg and to link with the Russian forces in the valley of the Danube. Our III, XII and XX Corps were to take part in this attack.

By 24 April, Third Army spearheads had reached a point twelve miles from Regensburg, which was an important outer bastion of the Southern Redoubt. Our troops now were only twenty miles from the Russian forces in Czechoslovakia. The next day we reached the Danube, only thirty-five miles from the Austrian border. Then the German government, through a Swiss intermediary, offered to leave all Allied prisoners behind as the German armies retreated. This offer was accepted by the United States, Britain and Russia. Just at this time the 99th Infantry Division (III Corps) liberated 20,000 prisoners, mostly American, at Moosburg.

On 26 April, at 0200, the 65th Infantry Division made an assault crossing of the Danube River and the next day the 71st Infantry Division followed. Not much enemy opposition was encountered as we approached the Danube, but all bridges were blown and the enemy was alert along the south bank of the river. In the western portion of Third Army, particularly in the III Corps zone, there was a decided increase in enemy resistance as the Altmuhl River line was reached and bridgeheads established. Our river crossings were hampered by artillery and mortar fire.

The next day the 11th Armored Division (XII Corps) advanced twenty miles and elements crossed the Austrian border. Some of our Danube crossings met small arms, mortar and artillery fire, but as our bridgeheads were expanded the resistance melted. At Abbach, elements of the 28th SS Grenadier Division, composed of Nazi youths of 16 and 17, fought fanatically.

The trend of enemy rail and motor traffic continued

south as General Patton's troops poured across the Danube and other of his columns drove farther into Austria. On 28 April the 65th Infantry Division (XX Corps) captured Regensburg, a city of 81,000. Our 13th Armored Division spearheads (XX Corps) were racing along the highways, encountering only scattered resistance in their advance to the Isar River, where two bridgeheads were established. Third Army forces were advancing on Munich. Fanatical attacks were made against the 14th Armored (III Corps) in its advance to the Isar River by young 16 to 18 year old Nazis of the 38th SS Grenadier Division.

On 29 April reports came to us from San Francisco, where the United Nations Conference was in session, that Germany had surrendered to the three major powers, but President Truman quickly declared the rumors unfounded.

By 1 May, Landau was cleared by the 71st Infantry Division (XX Corps), but there was stubborn enemy resistance against the 11th Armored in Austria and a serious counterattack was made against the 86th Infantry Division, which, however, was repulsed. Two days later General Patton's forces had broken across the river barrier in the Redoubt—the Isar—and continuing gains of ten to thirty miles were made by all divisions, motorized infantry as well as armored.

Third Army troops now were across the Inn River and were rapidly closing in on Salzburg and Berchtesgaden. Surrender of enemy forces in western Austria to the Seventh U. S. Army, however, kept us from taking these cities.

Other of General Patton's columns had driven within fifteen miles of Linz, third largest city of Austria, and the home of the Austrian branch of the Skoda munitions works.

Enemy disintegration was becoming more and more rapid. The curtain was falling on what was left of Hitler's Third Reich.

On 4 May, the V Corps was assigned to Third Army. As late as 5 May, 14 enemy planes were over the Third Army area, although on that same day one of the Nazis' most famous outfits, the 11th Panzer Division, surrendered intact. Next day the 11th Armored Division and the 26th Infantry Division (XII Corps) entered Linz, and the following day the 16th Armored (V Corps) advanced to Pilsen, as did the 9th Armored, which occupied it. On this same day, 7 May, a restraining line was placed on the Third Army. Only one enemy plane was over our entire zone as all units halted their advances.

On 8 May, VE Day was announced. The United Nations celebrated complete victory in Europe as all German air, land and sea forces surrendered unconditionally as of midnight.

During this last campaign, General Patton's Third Army captured 32,763 miles of enemy-held territory. That it did not advance even farther was due to restraining lines placed upon it from time to time by higher headquarters. Its losses were by far the lightest of any campaign in which the Third Army participated: 2,102 killed, 7,954 wounded and 1,591 missing, a total of 11,647. Against these losses of ours we killed an estimated 20,100 of the enemy, wounded 47,700, and took 653,140 prisoners, a total of enemy casualties in this last campaign of 720,940. By comparison the enemy losses were over 62 to 1.

Since the date on which it became operational in Normandy, 1 August, until 8 May, VE Day, the Third Army was in continuous combat for 281 days. It normally

●perated with a strength of between 250,000 and 400,000 men.   It crossed 24 major rivers and innumerable lesser streams, and under General Patton's infallible leadership, it advanced farther and faster than any other army in history.   In all it captured 81,500 square miles of territory and took more than 12,000 cities and towns.   It captured a grand total of 1,280,688 prisoners of war and it killed an estimated 144,500 and wounded an estimated 386,200 of the enemy.

15

Patton—The Man

WAR is a grim and tragic business. But until mankind plans and puts into effect some scheme of peacefully settling disagreements between nations, war is inevitable.

It behooves us to make the United Nations Organization really work, and to establish international law backed by *force*. A law not backed by force is not worth the paper upon which it is written.

Let me illustrate with an incident. I had a friend in the Reserve Corps a few years ago, in the days of peace when most of America was not worrying about war. He was a lawyer, and wanted to go to summer training camp, but he had a case coming up in court at the same time. He went to the Judge and asked for a postponement, giving his reason.

"Why are you wasting time in the Army?" the Judge asked. "We waste too much of the people's money on the army now. This case is far more important than your getting to camp. It cannot be postponed."

Just at that moment a court writ was handed to the Judge. He signed it and handed it to a court officer with orders to see that it was put into effect. The young lawyer again addressed the Judge.

"I do not mean to be impertinent, your Honor," he said, "but do you realize that, in the final analysis, the power or force to carry out the order which you have just signed, resides in the United States Army?"

The Judge looked at him a moment, then said: "I never have thought of it in just that way. Your case is postponed. You may go to camp."

Fortunately for America, when we were forced to go to war we had the combination of the three things necessary for victory. The first was a strong and patriotic young manhood, a "dogface" GI Joe, clever mentally and strong physically, who could swap blows with the craftiest war-trained Nazi and come out on top; the second was excellent equipment and plenty of it, produced by skillful labor and mangement at home and delivered to our men overseas; and the third was superb leadership—comprehensive over-all strategy and impeccable field tactics.

Among our field commanders, General George S. Patton, Jr., undoubtedly will go down in history as one of, if not the, greatest. Tall, trim and distinguished in appearance, with short-cropped, silvery hair, at 58 he was always an inspiring sight, particularly on any battlefield. The man breathed confidence and inspired men to the limit of their powers. He was always so *right* in all of his decisions. When he had once decided to do a certain thing, we could see immediately that it was the best and most sensible action, and we were confident that it would succeed.

It was fascinating to be present when the information from the various fronts was being presented in brief form, together with information relating to the air arm, and intelligence of the enemy. Frequently the General would ask questions or advice of members of his staff, particularly Major General Weyland, commanding the XIX Tactical Air Force, which was supporting us, or his Corps Commanders if they were present. And after he had heard everything he would say, in a few terse words: "We will do so and so ——. The Germans will think we are going to do so-and-so, but we will do this instead, by moving this division from here to here and sending this division here (pointing on the map). We will catch the bastards napping!" He would say it with a grin. And we always did. No matter what he said, it all appeared very simple and absolutely logical and we just knew it would work.

General Eisenhower visited our headquarters one day in March, 1945, and at the Staff meeting in the morning paid General Patton and the Third Army one of the finest compliments I have ever heard. He said, among other things:

"I warmly congratulate you, General Patton, and all your officers. Since last summer, when you became operational in Normandy, the Third Army has not made one mistake!"

General Patton was, I believe, a man absolutely without fear. I do not mean to imply that he was foolhardy, for he always took reasonable precautions, as any sensible man would. But he never spared himself, and he went wherever he felt his presence would help. He visited various sectors of the front practically every day, no matter what the weather, come hell or high water. Many times he would spend all day and much of the night visiting corps and front line divisions. Wherever the fighting was the heaviest or a new attack was to take place or a breakthrough was to be attempted—there the Old Man would be. No wonder the men worshiped him.

One day in early October, 1944, I "sent myself," so to speak, as I frequently did in lieu of one of the other Headquarters officers, to make a liaison visit to one of the front line divisions. It was the 4th Armored, commanded at that time, by Major General John S. Wood.

The 4th Armored was spearheading an attack against increasing German resistance several miles east of Nancy in the midst of hostile country. The whole division was on the move, Combat Commands A and B on different roads, with C.C.R. (the reserve) following closely behind.

Master Sergeant Corocci, who was driving my jeep, and I had spent an exciting few hours with the various columns, for they were well extended over several miles into enemy country. Several gun fights had been taking place, but our columns continued forward. I had contacted the various officers I had intended to and had gotten the necessary information to take back to our G-2 and G-3 Sections, when suddenly there was a heavy German counterattack, and 88's and mortar shells began coming from the flanks as well as the front. Our tanks moved rapidly off the roads and into position, and all the other vehicles moved under cover behind knolls or whatever shelter they could find. Some of our mechanized cavalry was driven back and the fight continued for an hour or so.

Then shells began falling all along the road on which we had traveled to the front—the only road which had been open to Nancy.

Just at that moment who should we see, coming up the road toward the front, but the Old Man himself, big as life, sitting up straight next to the driver in the front seat of his jeep with its top down, the three stars of a Lieutenant General showing clearly, and his only protection a 50-caliber machine gun mounted on the rear of the jeep, manned by one of his aides. It was a thrilling sight to see him travel right on up toward the very front through the shot and shell. And what a tonic it was to the officers and men who fought the Germans this way every day!

Another illustration of his freedom from fear was drawn one night in early August, just as the Third Army was breaking out of Normandy at Avranches. That was just at the narrow point of the eight-mile-wide gap and the Germans were trying desperately to close it by panzer attacks from the east and by continuous air attacks day and night. General Patton had ordered our Headquarters set up in several adjoining fields in the center of this gap, so that he could be right on the ground to see that all of our divisions were pushed through the opening quickly.

Our tents were under camouflage and the G-3 Section was just on the other side of a high dirt Normandy hedge row from the Chief of Staff's and the General's trailers, which also were under camouflage.

Just after dark—almost midnight—Jerry came over in force and began to bomb the vital bridges, ammunition dumps, troop concentrations and headquarters. First they placed two large green lights, or lanterns, as we called them, one on each side of the area to be bombed, and then a central red lantern as a bullseye. Then the bombers came over, by the hundreds it seemed, and laid their eggs. You could hear them whistle and scream as they fell and the ground rocked with the explosions. The planes circled over for more than an hour, sounding like a great hive of angry hornets.

As soon as the bombing began, all lights were extinguished in all our tents, even in the G-3 operations tent, so the blackout was complete. Many who did not have vital work to do at the time crouched close to the high earthen banks of the hedgerows between the fields, seeking some protection from bomb splinters. For many of our young officers, it was almost their first combat and certainly the worst they had experienced.

At the height of the bombing there was a call in the darkness for me, as the Chief Liaison Officer. An officer from a Corps headquarters had arrived with a secret message in a sealed envelope for General Patton. I walked with the corps officer over to the opening in the earth hedgerow which led into the field where the trailers of the General and his Chief of Staff were and took him to the Chief of Staff. The Chief directed that the officer deliver his letter in person to the General and I left.

When the corps officer returned to my tent and was

ready to leave, I asked him what General Patton had been doing when he reached him during the heavy bombing.

"He was sitting there in a deck chair," the officer replied, "in the field a little way from his trailer. He was smoking a cigar and looking up into the sky, all lit up with Jerry's lanterns, watching the bombing. I was nervous and perspiring and jumpy," the officer went on, "but the General was cool as a cucumber. He just looked up into the sky and kept saying aloud: "Those (g—d— b—s), those rotten sons-of-b—s! We'll get them! We'll get them;' "

Then the corps officer added: "Well, if our Chief isn't any more afraid of the Heinie bombers than that, I guess I shouldn't be either." And he walked away into the noisy darkness.

But again I say, General Patton wasn't foolhardy. Next day he ordered Third Army Headquarters moved down into the open country below Avranches, out of the bottle-neck.

The General was an immaculate dresser, even under the worst possible weather conditions. His leather and brass were always polished and his clothes neatly cleaned and pressed. If he got muddy or wet at the front, as he often did, he changed immediately upon his return to Headquarters. He insisted always on his Staff being well-dressed, also. His own helmet was always shellacked and shining and he always wore side arms, frequently his beloved pearl-handled pistols, with which he was an expert. And he usually wore, or at least carried, his gloves.

General Patton's philosophy about life and war was very clear and sane and logical. He deplored war and all its misery and pain and death, but as long as there was war, the only thing to do was to win it as quickly as possible and with the fewest casualties on our side.

If one of his commanders sustained what he considered an undue number of casualties among his officers and men, General Patton would relieve him on the spot. Many commanders were relieved for this reason. The casualties of the Third Army, compared to other armies on the basis of accomplishment, were surprisingly small.

When a new unit, not having had any previous combat experience, first entered the front line under the Third Army, General Patton had it first placed, not necessarily on a quiet front, as there were comparatively few of those, but on a front where it could take its place between two battle-seasoned units. And he placed it, if possible, in a sector in which we were winning at the time and pushing forward. He wanted it to get a taste of victory and to gain confidence. And when he first put a unit in the line, he always had an experienced unit in reserve close behind it, so that if a serious counterattack should take place, the seasoned unit was there to help stop it.

This first experience of a division or other unit on the front was called "getting a bloody nose." Some men were bound to be killed and some wounded, but as few as possible, and the whole unit got its first battle experience and also its confidence and the feel of conquering.

General Patton was a great psychologist. His ability to size up a difficult situation and then to bring about the necessary action by his own forces at the desired point, was uncanny.

General Patton used to say to his divisions before they entered battle something like this:

"Men, this stuff some sources sling around about America wanting to stay out of the war and not wanting to fight is a lot of baloney. Americans love to fight, traditionally. All real Americans love the thrill and clash of battle. You are here today for three reasons. First, you are here to defend your homes and loved ones; second, you are here for your own self-respect, because you wouldn't want to be anywhere else; and third, because you are real men and all real men like to fight. Americans play to win. That's why America has never lost and never will lose a war, for the very thought of losing is hateful to an American.

"You are not all going to die. Only two per cent of you right here today would be killed in a major battle. Death must not be feared. Death in time comes to all of us, and every man is scared in his first action. If he says he's not, he's a damn liar. Some men are cowards, yes, but they fight just the same or get the hell slammed out of them. The real hero is the man who fights even though he is scared. Some get over their fright in a minute under fire. Others take an hour. For some it takes days, but a real man will never let the fear of death overpower his honor, his sense of duty to his country or his manhood."

And with all his rough talk, he was kind and solicitous about the needs of his men. He would relieve in an instant any commander who did not take care of his men and see that they had the best equipment, clothing and food available, and as many comforts as possible at the front. He believed, above all, however, that morale was kept up best by winning, no matter what the hardships.

One time during the miserably cold, rainy weather of November, when everything was a sea of mud and the men's feet were being frost-bitten as we pushed the difficult fighting beyond the Moselle River and the Saar Valley, I was visiting a front line infantry division (the 90th.) The conditions were really frightful as the men prowled through deserted houses and villages looking for snipers and mopping up as they went along. It was at this time that one of our doughboys said to his officer: "Lieutenant, is France all just mud and cow manure?"

On this trip I noticed that, despite the mud and rain and cold, the men seemed very cheerful. When I returned to Headquarters that evening, I said to Colonel Paul Harkins, our deputy Chief of Staff: "Paul, how in the devil can our GIs remain so cheerful at the front under these frightful winter conditions?" Colonel Harkins replied: "Well, the Old Man knows that as long as they are winning and moving forward they will be happy and their morale will be high. That's the reason he wants to keep moving and winning all through the winter."

That was one of his favorite theories—keep moving forward. He used to tell his divisions not to dig in, but to keep moving forward. He would say: "Dig in and you are dead! You will be a perfect target for the enemy mortars. If you keep moving forward you will be a more difficult target for the enemy and he will be more nervous and unsteady in his aim, because you are getting closer and closer to him for the kill."

He believed and preached the same theory about invading across the beaches. One day in England, before the invasion, he was asked to speak before a large group of British officers, and he expounded his theory about keeping moving across the beaches. He said: "Of course, you British have had experience in landing on beaches, in the last war, at Gallipoli. The trouble is, most of you are still there!"

The British officers got the point and thoroughly enjoyed it. The British, as a rule, were great admirers of General Patton and he got tremendous attention in the English newspapers.

Many persons have the impression that General Patton was just a daredevil type of commander, who took long chances and won because he was lucky. I might observe that the telephone code name for Third Army Headquarters was the word LUCKY, but it was far more than luck that made General Patton always win.

There never was a field commander who gathered more detailed information about his enemy before he launched an attack, or who had more detailed studies made of the terrain over which he was to attack. Information from every available source was collected, sifted, checked and counter-checked. G-2 reports from SHAEF and Twelfth Army Group were scanned for all information about enemy divisions moving from the Russian front, and from points as far away as Norway and Denmark. He knew about how long it would take to bring a division from these various points, and he wanted to guard against a surprise attack on one of his flanks. He would not start an attack until the location of every enemy division was accounted for.

Most thorough and detailed reports were made, as I have said, on all of the terrain to be covered. The weather forecasts were checked and of course our own supply situation. Then the condition and quality of our own equipment and finally the condition and morale of our own troops. Absolutely nothing was left to chance.

The Old Man apparently made his decisions very rapidly, but they always were based on the fullest information and data prepared by his staff. After his decision was made, then the detailed plans were worked out with the most minute care, so that his decisions could be carried out. These plans were continuing and ever-changing with the fluidity of the situation, but they were never based on a hunch or a long chance. They were executed so rapidly, however, that to the public they probably did appear frequently as long chances. Patton's thrusts were the bane of the German High Command. He did things so well and so rapidly that to them he was unpredictable.

As a final tribute to him at the time of his death, General Eisenhower stated of General Patton: "He was one of those men born to be a soldier, an ideal combat leader whose gallantry and dramatic personality inspired all he commanded to great deeds of valor. His presence gave me the certainty that the boldest plan would be even more daringly executed.

"It is no exaggeration to say that Patton's name struck terror at the hearts of the enemy."

One of the first principles of warfare always has been to "guard your flanks." During one of the Third Army's many long dashes into enemy-infested country, a visiting General once said to General Patton: "Georgie, aren't you worried about your flanks? Are they protected?" General Patton replied: "The hell with my flanks. I'm going to make the Heinies worry about theirs."

Actually, however, he did carefully watch his flanks, but he did it in the modern way, with his direct-support air forces. There never was a great commander who worked closer with his air forces. The XIX Tactical Air Force did a magnificent job in giving not only superior air-ground support, but also in perfect reconnaissance on the flanks and miles to the front into enemy territory. And General Patton always appreciated and gave credit to its services.

During the campaigns, I used frequently to think of Napoleon's formula for military success, and realize how it applied to General Patton. Napoleon said: "To be successful in battle, a commander must concentrate his forces, preserve the initiative, and resolve to die rather than to retreat."

Some might at first think that General Patton scattered his forces all over France, but actually they were concentrated in great strength, at several points instead of one, and they moved with such great speed and power that they confused and confounded the enemy.

Another of General Patton's sayings was: "If you want an army to fight and risk death, you've got to get up there and lead it. An army is like spaghetti. You can't push a piece of spaghetti, you've got to pull it!"

Again he said many times at the front: "We have only one job over here, and that is to kill Germans. When we have killed enough Germans, the war will be over. Then we can all go home." How true this turned out to be!

And again he used to say: "There are only three principles of warfare—Audacity, *Audacity*, AUDACITY!"

One of Patton's most pungent and illustrative observations was in regard to his method of attack. He would first attack all along his front, so that the enemy was completely engaged and forced to bring up his reserves. Then Patton would find a soft spot in their defenses and, as planned, would push an armored division, accompanied by motorized infantry, through the opening. These troops would have instructions to push clear through to the enemy rear areas, possibly a river line, and not till then to turn either right or left, to cut all the enemy communications, capture their supplies and then turn back to the main line of battle to form the other jaw of a vise. This would cut the enemy completely to pieces and we could capture what was left of them. General Patton always said that it was very simple: "You just grab them by the nose and kick them in the pants!"

Much has been written and spoken about the famous so-called "slapping incident" in Sicily. General Patton never said one word in his own defense, but for the record, here is the true story as told to me by one who was there.

The General, as has been mentioned, was a great one to look after the welfare of his men and to see that they were well taken care of, especially the wounded and the sick. He made frequent visits to the hospitals.

After the Sicilian campaign, where a minimum of casualties had been incurred considering all that his Seventh Army had accomplished, he went one day to visit the wounded in one of the large hospitals. He spent the whole afternoon going through the wards, chatting with the men and cheering them up.

As he came to the last ward, having been much upset and distressed by the sights he had seen of the severely wounded and having seen how bravely they held to their morale and their courage despite their pain and the dark future which many faced, suddenly he saw a young soldier sitting on the edge of his cot, apparently crying. General Patton went over to him and said: "What is wrong with you, soldier? Are you hurt?"

Without rising, but burying his face in his hands, the soldier wimpered: "Oh, no, I'm not hurt, but oh, it's terrible—terrible—boo-hoo-hoo!"

With that the General, perfectly disgusted after seeing all the badly wounded and mutilated soldiers, commanded: "Stand up!" The soldier got to his feet and General Patton took his leather gloves which he was carrying and slapped him across the neck, and said: "Why don't you act like a man instead of a g—— d—— snivelling baby? Look at all those severely wounded soldiers, not complaining a bit and cheerful as can be, and here you are, a damn yellow crybaby!"

I was told by a medical officer later, in Washington, that it was the best thing that could have happened to the boy, and that he was discharged from the hospital in less than a week, perfectly normal and well.

But the story eventually reached a columnist in Washington and he, realizing that General Patton was a great general and a very prominent person, painted the tale in lurid colors and it spread all over the United States. Fortunately, General Eisenhower was big enough and a keen enough judge of men to realize that General Patton was one of his best commanders, and even with a certain amount of peril to his own position because of the public furor, placed him in command of the Third Army, so that together they made military history.

Some persons may not have realized the intensity of the passions aroused over the garbling of this tale, or the blind, unreasoning detestation for a great American soldier that was created. One day in Washington, after V-E Day, I was taken by an Army officer friend to call upon a Congressman. While we waited, the officer introduced me to the Congressman's secretary with the added remark: "Colonel Wallace was on General Patton's staff."

Instantly the girl replied: "Oh, I don't like General Patton. I just hate him. He hits wounded soldiers!" I said, "Would you like to hear the real story of that incident?" "No," she answered, "I don't want to hear anything about him. I just hate him for hitting that soldier."

My officer friend, a little annoyed by then, ended the conversation by saying: "Well, don't get excited about it, sister. The Germans didn't like him, either."

General Patton, to his own detriment, frequently was not tactful. No one could accuse him of being a diplomat, but the man was so frank that he just couldn't help saying what he knew to be the truth. He had the rare gift of being able to use words that were so absolutely descriptive, and he said things in such a succinct way, that they frequently startled and shocked people, but no one ever failed to get his meaning. His words were few, but they were like sharp knives which quickly stripped a subject of all sham and left the naked truth for all to see. He became so famous, he spoke so seldom, and his remarks frequently were so incisive or amusing that anything and everything he did say was flashed all over the world. Most of the things he said that drew criticism could have been said by any other general officer and little attention would have been paid to them, but in Patton's colorful phraseology they got wide circulation.

One day in late October, 1944, the Chief of Staff, General George C. Marshall visited our Headquarters at Etain, France, a town of medium size about ten miles east of Verdun. During the First World War, all the buildings were destroyed and the German High Command had an underground headquarters below the foundations of the old buildings. During the last great Battle of Verdun, when the Germans felt sure they were going to take the fortress city, the Kaiser was brought to that headquarters on the first day to be close enough to witness the jump-off. He was assured that this time his army would capture Verdun and the soldiers were told of his presence to inspire them. It is, of course, history that Verdun did not fall, and after three days of watching the stream of German wounded coming back through Etain, the Kaiser got discouraged and left.

Well, 28 years later our Third Army Headquarters was set up in the town and there General Marshall attended a special briefing with General Patton and his Section Chiefs in the war room, where the big operations maps were, in a large barn on an estate. After the briefing, which General Marshall followed with obvious interest, he asked General Patton a number of questions. When these had been answered satisfactorily, the Chief of Staff said:

"Well, George, you are doing a grand job. Now, is there anything I can have sent over to you, or anything I can do for you?"

With his grin spreading from ear to ear Patton said:

"Yes, there is one thing you can do for me and all this fine staff of mine, General. After we have finished up over here, you can send us all to the Pacific to clean up those little yellow bastards over there!"

Everybody laughed, including General Marshall who replied with a smile: "Georgie, we'll see about that later. Let's get this job finished up first."

General Marshall thought very highly of General Patton and his abilities and his tribute is quoted:

"He was one of the greatest military leaders in our history."

"In the fighting in Africa and in Sicily, he was conspicuous for the driving energy and tactical skill with which he led his troops.

"The breakthrough of the Third Army in Normandy and its dramatic liberation of central France was indicative of the man who led it.

"But it was his counterattack toward Bastogne and the tremendous thrust to the Rhine at Coblenz and into the center and rear of the German armies in the Saar Basin, followed by the sudden crossing of the Rhine, that established General Patton as one of the greatest military leaders in our history."

We who lived and worked at Third Army Headquarters through those great days have many tragic memories, but also many treasured ones, which will grow richer as time passes.

Certainly not least of these will be wrapped about the recollections of our daily association with one whom we all came to recognize as not only a great general but also a great man, an association which broadened our horizons and colored and enriched our lives, both at the time and for the years to come.

There never was a dull moment while serving under General Patton. He was a showman, yes, but he was far more than that. He was the greatest field commander of our time. Anyone who ever worked closely with him would have died for him, and soldiers in the Third Army loved, respected and admired him.

Upon his visit to America, during the summer of 1945, he paid a tribute to the soldiers he commanded, when, standing at attention before some wounded veterans during a special ceremony held for him at Boston, he declared: "The great honor you do me belongs to the veterans of the Third Army. I salute them!"

As one of the men whom he had commanded said at the time of his tragic death: "There'll never be another Army commander like him."

He had one of the keenest senses of humor of any man I ever knew, and this, coupled with his brilliant mind, made all on his staff love to work for him. He was an inspiring leader and got the best out of all who worked for him and he never hesitated to give credit to subordinates where credit was due. He had a genius for inspiring those under him to do better than their best. Under him, difficult things seemed easy and hardships became almost a pleasure.

While working for him you instinctively felt an atmosphere of greatness about him. He never did unnecessary things. He always saw the important things and grasped the broad aspect of impending events. In all of his campaigns he rarely, if ever, made a mistake. He never retreated. He always won.

General Patton was innately a deeply religious man. Despite his at times rough talk and his great strength and force, he was very kind and quite emotional. In the field he attended religious services regularly, but he liked neither sham nor show in his worship.

When he first came to his Headquarters at Peover (pronounced Peever) Hall, Knutsford, in England, I, having been in England for many months, was sent there as Liaison Officer to greet the advance party of Third Army Headquarters and indoctrinate them in the customs and methods of the United States Army overseas, particularly in our relations with the British. This was shortly before I was asked to become a permanent member of the Third Army staff.

The Headquarters was located in the large, old and very interesting manor house called Peover Hall, dating back to the fourteenth century. The grounds of the estate had remained in possession of one family, the Manwarings, for about 800 years. The Manwarings were closely related to the famous Peel family. For countless years fox-hunters started the chase from this old hall, and Old John Peel, about whom was written the famous hunting song "John Peel", probably hunted there.

When the first Sunday arrived, the General's senior aide, Colonel Charles R. Codman, asked me if I knew anything about the churches in the neighborhood. He said he had looked over several in the town, but thought the General would be better pleased with something simpler. I asked Colonel Codman if he had looked at the private chapel on the estate. He said he did not know there was one, so I took him back and showed him.

This chapel was one of the most interesting and beautiful I have ever seen. For hundreds of years it had been the private place of worship for the Manwaring and Peel families and also the families of those who worked on the estate. The interior was lined with tombs of knights and their ladies, and on top of each tomb, or recessed within the walls, were life-size figures of the dead. Each knight's head rested on the neck of his horse and his feet against the body of his favorite dog, all in lifelike marble.

Colonel Codman thought the General would like the chapel and asked me to join them for the service. It was a bitterly cold January day and about as cold inside the chapel as out. We could see our breaths and kept our trench coats on.

The service was extremely simple, and the rector himself came down and gave us hymnals. It was Communion Sunday and when it came our turn, General Patton rose and went forward. We followed and all knelt at the altar and took Communion.

Soon after the service I asked Colonel Codman if the General had been displeased by anything about the service. He replied, not in the least, that the General had enjoyed its simple sincerity. From that day on he was a regular attendant at the services until we moved on in June.

After we moved, General Patton had a simple bronze tablet made and presented it to the chapel, along with an American flag. The tablet, now embedded in the chapel wall, bears only these words: "Presented by Headquarters, Third U. S. Army, January-June, 1944."

May God grant that war be outlawed, and may it never come to our land again. But if it ever should, God grant that another Patton may appear to lead our soldiers as magnificently and as perfectly as they were led in this war by General George Smith Patton, Jr.

May his spirit live again.

APPENDIX I

THIRD U. S. ARMY

CHRONOLOGICAL RECORD OF EVENTS

1 January 1944 to 8 May 1945

1 Jan 44—Third U. S. Army, at Fort Sam Houston, Texas alerted for overseas duty.

26 Jan 44—XV Corps assigned Third U. S. Army.

29 Jan 44—Advance Detachment, Headquarters Third U. S. Army arrived at Peover Hall, Knutsford, Cheshire, England.

27 Feb 44—XX Corps assigned to Third U. S. Army.

12 Mar 44—Headquarters Third U. S. Army boarded Ile de France in New York harbor for overseas voyage.

13 Mar 44—VIII Corps assigned Third U. S. Army.

21 Mar 44—The Ile de France reached Greenock, Scotland.

23 Mar 44—Forward Echelon, Headquarters Third U. S. Army set up at Peover Hall, while Rear Echelon arrived at Camp Toft, 1 mile away.

25 Mar 44—Headquarters welcomed by Lt. Gen. G. S. Patton, Jr., new Army Commander.

31 Mar 44—XII Corps assigned Third U. S. Army.

6 Jun 44—D-Day—VIII Corps attached for operations to First U. S. Army.

28 Jun 44—Headquarters moved south, Forward Echelon to Breamore House, and Rear Echelon to Nine Yews, both south of Salisbury, England.

4 Jul 44—Boarded boats for shipment to France.

215

Appendix I

6 July 44—Arrived at Nehou, France where Headquarters set up under canvas for the first time.

1 Aug 44—Third U. S. Army became operational at 1200 with VIII and XV Corps. VIII Corps released from attachment to First U. S. Army. Attack to the south from Avranches. XIX Tactical Air Command became operational—in cooperation with Third U. S. Army. Headquarters Third U. S. Army moved from Nehou to Bingard, northeast of Coutances.

2 Aug 44—Headquarters Third U. S. Army moved to Beauchamps.

3 Aug 44—VIII Corps started west into Brittany toward Brest while XV Corps cut to the east.

5 Aug 44—Vannes and Laval captured.

7 Aug 44—XX Corps became operational.

8 Aug 44—Le Mans captured; St. Malo under attack. Headquarters Third U. S. Army moved to Poilley, near Fougeres.

10 Aug 44—Angers cleared.

12 Aug 44—XII Corps became operational. Headquarters Third U. S. Army moved to Andonville, near Laval.

13 Aug 44—XV Corps reached Argentan in its drive to the north to close southern jaw of Falaise Gap.

15 Aug 44—Headquarters Third U. S. Army moved to La Bocage, near Le Mans.

16 Aug 44—Chateaudun, Dreux, Chartres, Orleans captured.

17 Aug 44—All resistance at St. Malo ceased.

19 Aug 44—Bridgehead over Seine secured at Mantes-Gassicourt—drive to north to Vernon to cut off German escape route across Seine River.

20 Aug 44—Headquarters Third U. S. Army moved to Brou.

APPENDIX I

21 Aug 44—Sens, Etampes secured.

23 Aug 44—Fontainbleau and Montargis fell. XV Corps passed to control of First U. S. Army.

25 Aug 44—Troyes cleared. Major assault on Brest commenced. Headquarters Third U. S. Army moved to Vrigny, south of Pithiviers.

26 Aug 44—Chateau-Thierry and Nogent-Sur-Seine cleared.

29 Aug 44—Reims, Chalons-Sur-Marne, Vitry le Francois, Montmirall, Epernay taken. XV Corps reverted to control of Third U. S. Army.

30 Aug 44—Headquarters Third U. S. Army moved to La Chaume, east of Sens.

31 Aug 44—Verdun captured.

4 Sep 44—Headquarters Third U. S. Army moved to L'Pine, east of Chalons-Sur-Marne.

5 Sep 44—VIII Corps passed to Ninth U. S. Army.

8 Sep 44—First crossing of the Moselle River.

15 Sep 44—Nancy cleared. Headquarters Third U. S. Army moved to Braquis, south of Etain.

22 Sep 44—Headquarters Third U. S. Army moved to Etain.

25 Sep 44—Third U. S. Army ordered to assume aggressive defense because of acute supply situation.

29 Sep 44—XV Corps passed to Seventh U. S. Army.

2 Oct 44—Attack began on Fort Driant, a Metz fortress.

10 Oct 44—III Corps assigned Third U. S. Army.

11 Oct 44—Headquarters Third U. S. Army moved to Nancy.

13 Oct 44—Task Force Warnock withdrew from Fort Driant.

30 Oct 44—Maizieres-Les-Metz cleared.

8 Nov 44—XII Corps attacked to the east.

9 Nov 44—XX Corps opened its converging attack on Metz.

22 Nov 44—Metz cleared.
23 Nov 44—First crossing of Saar River in XII Corps zone.
27 Nov 44—St. Avold taken.
6 Dec 44—Fort St. Quentin fell.
8 Dec 44—Fort Driant taken.
11 Dec 44—Sarreguemines captured.
13 Dec 44—Fort Jeanne D'Arc captured—all resistance around Metz ceased.
16 Dec 44—Breakthrough of enemy in First U. S. Army zone.
18 Dec 44—Third U. S. Army ordered to swing north toward enemy breakthrough area.
20 Dec 44—Advance Detachment, Headquarters Third U. S. Army moved from Nancy to Luxembourg.
21 Dec 44—VIII Corps came to control of Third U. S. Army.
26 Dec 44—Contact made by 4th Armored Division with 101st Airborne Division outside of Bastogne.
27 Dec 44—Remainder of Forward Echelon, Headquarters Third U. S. Army moved from Nancy to Luxembourg.
11 Jan 45—St. Hubert cleared.
14 Jan 45—Contact with British made on western end of enemy breakthrough area.
16 Jan 45—Contact made with First U. S. Army near Houffalize.
11 Feb 45—III Corps passed to First U. S. Army.
12 Feb 45—Prum cleared.
22 Feb 45—Moselle-Saar Triangle cleared.
26 Feb 45—Bitburg taken.
2 Mar 45—Trier taken.
5 Mar 45—Dash to the Rhine from Kyll River.
9 Mar 45—Rhine River reached.

13 Mar 45—Moselle crossed as forces drove into Saar Industrial region.

13 Mar 45—Coblenz, Bad Kreuznach, Bingen, St. Wendel, Dillingen cleared.

20 Mar 45—Worms, Kaiserslautern captured.

22 Mar 45—Mainz and Landau captured.

23 Mar 45—First assault crossing of Rhine—Speyer and Ludwigshafen captured.

25 Mar 45—Darmstadt cleared.

27 Mar 45—Headquarters Third U. S. Army moved from Luxembourg to Idar-Oberstein. Hanau captured.

28 Mar 45—Wiesbaden taken.

29 Mar 45—Frankfurt cleared—attack to the north.

3 Apr 45—Headquarters Third U. S. Army moved from Idar-Oberstein to Frankfurt.

4 Apr 45—Kassel, Muhlhausen, Gotha cleared.

5 Apr 45—Eisenach, Meiningen captured.

11 Apr 45—Headquarters Third U. S. Army moved from Frankfurt to Hersfeld. Weimar taken.

12 Apr 45—Erfurt cleared.

13 Apr 45—Jena and Zeitz captured.

14 Apr 45—Bayreuth and Gera taken.

15 Apr 45—Hof, Glauchau, Crimmitschau, Plauen captured.

17 Apr 45—Forces switched to attack south in new zone.

18 Apr 45—III Corps reverted to Third U. S. Army.

22 Apr 45—Last campaign of war begins. Headquarters Third U. S. Army moved to Erlangen. VIII Corps passed to First U. S. Army.

25 Apr 45—Danube River crossed.

27 Apr 45—Regensburg captured.

29 Apr 45—Landshut and Moosburg cleared—Isar River crossed.

1 May 45—Inn River crossed—Army forces in Austria in strength.

APPENDIX I

2 May 45—Headquarters Third U. S. Army moved to Regensburg.

4 May 45—Linz taken.

5 May 45—Pilsen captured.

6 May 15—V Corps passed to Army control.

7 May 45—Announcement of surrender of all German air, sea and land forces to be effective at 0001 9 May 1945.

APPENDIX II

THIRD ARMY UNITS AND COMMANDERS

The Third U. S. Army had six corps which operated under the Army as follows:

Corps	Time	Number of Days
XII	1 August 1944–8 May 1945	281
XX	1 August 1944–8 May 1945	281
VIII	1 August 1944–5 September 1944 21 December 1944–22 April 1945	160
III	10 October 1944–11 February 1945 18 April 1945–8 May 1945	157
XV	1 August 1944–24 August 1944 29 August 1944–29 September 1944	56
V	6 May 1945–8 May 1945	3

The following five divisions were with Third U. S. Army more than the others, and all of them went through practically all of the heavy fighting in which the Army figured:

	Approximate Days
4th Armored Division	280
5th Infantry Division	276
80th Infantry Division	274
90th Infantry Division	272
6th Armored Division	252

III CORPS	V CORPS
Lt. Gen. John Millikin	Lt. Gen. Leonard T. Gerow
VIII CORPS	Maj. Gen.
Lt. Gen. Troy H. Middleton	Clarence R. Heubner

221

APPENDIX II

XV CORPS
Lt. Gen. Wade H. Haislip

XII CORPS
Lt. Gen. Manton S. Eddy

XX CORPS
Lt. Gen. Walton H. Walker

1st Infantry Div.	4th Armored Div.	76th Infantry Div.
2nd Infantry Div.	5th Armored Div.	79th Infantry Div.
4th Infantry Div.	6th Armored Div.	80th Infantry Div.
5th Infantry Div.	7th Armored Div.	83rd Infantry Div.
8th Infantry Div.	8th Armored Div.	86th Infantry Div.
26th Infantry Div.	9th Armored Div.	87th Infantry Div.
28th Infantry Div.	10th Armored Div.	89th Infantry Div.
29th Infantry Div.	11th Armored Div.	90th Infantry Div.
35th Infantry Div.	12th Armored Div.	94th Infantry Div.
65th Infantry Div.	13th Armored Div.	95th Infantry Dv.
69th Infantry Div.	14th Armored Div.	97th Infantry Div.
70th Infantry Div.	16th Armored Div.	99th Infantry Div.
71st Infantry Div.	20th Armored Div.	

2nd French Armd. Div.
17th Airborne Div.
101st Airborne Division

APPENDIX III

THE BASTOGNE SURRENDER ULTIMATUM AND REPLY

EXTRACT FROM G-2 PERIODIC REPORT— HEADQUARTERS VIII CORPS 30 December 1944

To the U S A Commander of the encircled town of Bastogne:

The fortune of war is changing. This time the U S A forces in and near Bastogne have been encircled by strong German armored units. More German armored units have crossed the river Our near Ortheuville, have taken Marche and reached St Hubert by passing through Homeres-Sibret-Tillet. Librimont is in German hands.

There is only one possibility to save the encircled U S A troops from total annihilation: that is the honorable surrender of the encircled town. In order to think it over, a term of two hours will be granted beginning with the presentation of this note.

If this proposal should be rejected, one German Arty Corps and six heavy AA Battalions are ready to annihilate the U S A Troops in and near Bastogne. The order of firing will be given immediately after this two hour's term.

All the serious civilian losses caused by this artillery fire would not correspond with the well-known American humanity.

The German Commander.

The German Commander received the following reply:

To the German Commander:

NUTS!

The American Commander.

223

APPENDIX IV. A TYPICAL CASUALTY REPORT FROM THE THIRD ARMY

SECRET

HEADQUARTERS THIRD U. S. ARMY

G-1 SECTION

DAILY CASUALTY REPORT NO. 287

CASUALTY REPORT TO 2400, 14 MAY 45

	DAILY CASUALTIES, 24-72 PD, 14 MAY				Cumulative Casualties			Reinforcements		Effective Strength as of 14 May 45
	T/O Strength	Battle	Non-Battle	Total	Battle	Non-Battle	Total	Daily	Cumulative	
1 Inf Div	14189	0	15	15	15003	13960	28963	0	23390	14472
2 Inf Div	14189	0	24	24	15066	10734	25800	0	21726	14565
4 Inf Div	14189	0	8	8	22454	13054	35508	5	36838	14559
5 Inf Div	14189	0	25	25	12510	10954	23464	0	23660	14660
9 Inf Div	14189	0	4	4	18631	15222	33853	0	34387	14700
26 Inf Div	14189	0	15	15	9960	6830	16790	0	17382	14693
65 Inf Div	14189	0	32	32	1052	1143	2195	550	3169	14532
71 Inf Div	14189	0	40	40	787	980	1767	43	2242	14187
80 Inf Div	14189	0	28	28	14533	10929	25462	2	25230	14624
90 Inf Div	14189	0	21	21	18460	9099	27559	0	27753	14683
97 Inf Div	14189	0	12	12	934	363	1297	0	1420	14168
99 Inf Div	14189	0	20	20	6103	5812	11915	260	11209	14525
474 Inf Regt	3207	0	0	0	4	141	145	0	285	3231
Sub-Total	173475	0	244	244	135497	99221	234718	860	228752	177599

4 Armd Div	10723	0	7	7	5968	4498	10486	311	11036	11626
9 Armd Div	10723	0	2	2	3952	1395	5347	0	6449	11149
11 Armd Div	10723	0	11	11	3216	1880	5096	0	5745	10793
13 Armd Div	10723	0	3	3	493	232	725	46	1047	10963
14 Armd Div	10723	0	7	7	2896	1372	4268	3	3579	10950
16 Armd Div	10723	0	14	14	12	197	209	0	586	11112
Sub-Total	64338	0	44	44	16537	9574	26131	360	28442	66593
TOTAL	237813	0	288	288	152034	108795	260849	1220	257194	244192

OUR OWN TROOPS

	14 May	Cumulative from 1 Aug. 44	Present Operation (Beg. 22 Apr. 45)
Killed	0	21482	385
Wounded	0	99262	2080
Missing	0	16154	57
Total	0	136898	2522
Non-Battle	374	113614	6911
GRAND TOTAL	374	250512	9433
Reinforcements .	1277	265095	20434

ENEMY TROOPS

Actual

	14 May	Cumulative from 1 Aug. 44	Present Operation (Beg. 22 Apr. 45)
Prisoners of War	291	1280979	737458
Enemy Buried ..	10	26575	271
Total	301	1307554	737729

Estimated

Prisoners	0	981000	436800
Killed	0	144500	5800
Wounded	0	386200	16500
Total	0	1511700	459100

MATERIAL LOST, CAPTURED AND DESTROYED

UNIT LOSSES

	14 May	Cumulative from 1 Aug. 44	Present Operation (Beg. 22 Apr. 45)
1. Tanks light ..	0	308	10
2. Tanks, Med. ..	0	949	15
3. Art. 75 mm or over	0	175	1
4. Vehicles, Total all types	0	3951	96
Total	0	5383	122

ENEMY CAPTURED OR DESTROYED

	14 May	Cumulative from 1 Aug. 44	Present Operation (Beg. 22 Apr. 45)
1. Tanks Mark 3-4	0	1533	41
2. Tanks Mark VI	0	862	5
3. Art. 75 mm and over	0	3460	136
4. Vehicles, Total all types	0	14396	1487
Total	0	20251	1669

Appendix IV

ENEMY AIRCRAFT DESTROYED

	14 May	Cumulative from 1 Aug. 44	Present Operation (Beg. 22 Apr. 45)
Category No. 1	0	1072	128
Category No. 2	0	566	61
Total	0	1638	139

APPENDIX V
HEADQUARTERS
THIRD UNITED STATES ARMY

APO 403

GENERAL ORDERS   1 January 1945
NUMBER 1

TO THE OFFICERS AND MEN OF THE THIRD ARMY AND TO OUR COMRADES OF THE XIX TACTICAL AIR COMMAND

From the bloody corridor at Avranches, to Brest, thence across France to the Saar, over the Saar into Germany, and now on to Bastogne, your record has been one of continuous victory. Not only have you invariably defeated a cunning and ruthless enemy, but also you have overcome by your indomitable fortitude every aspect of terrain and weather. Neither heat nor dust nor floods nor snow have stayed your progress. The speed and brilliancy of your achievements is unsurpassed in military history.

Recently I had the honor of receiving at the hands of the Twelfth Army Group Commander, Lieutenant General Omar N. Bradley, a second Oak Leaf Cluster to the DSM. This award was bestowed on me not for what I have done, but because of what you have achieved. From the bottom of my heart I thank you.

My New Year wish and sure conviction for you is that under the protection of Almighty God and the inspired leadership of our President and the High Command, you will continue your victorious course to the end that tyranny and vice shall be eliminated, our dead comrades avenged, and peace restored to a war-weary world.

Appendix V

In closing, I can find no fitter expression for my feelings than to apply to you the immortal words spoken by General Scott at Chapultepec when he said: "Brave soldiers, veterans, you have been baptized in fire and blood and have come out steel."

G. S. Patton, Jr.,
Lieut. General, U. S. Army,
Commanding.

DISTRIBUTION:
"A" & "C"
Twelfth Army Group
XIX TAC

APPENDIX VI
HEADQUARTERS
THIRD UNITED STATES ARMY
APO 403

26 January 1945

SUBJECT: Commendation.

TO: Officers and Men of the General and Special Staff, Third Army, APO 403, U. S. Army.

1. The almost incredible results achieved by the Third Army in the current operation were only possible through the superlatively good staff work existing throughout.

2. On behalf of myself and all the combat troops involved, I desire to express my sincere thanks and appreciation.

3. Each and everyone of you is hereby highly commended for your superior performance.

G. S. PATTON, JR.,
Lieut. General, U. S. Army,
Commanding.

APPENDIX VII
THE CHRISTMAS MESSAGE AND PRAYER SENT THE THIRD ARMY, 1944

HEADQUARTERS
THIRD UNITED STATES ARMY

To each officer and soldier in the Third United States Army, I wish a Merry Christmas. I have full confidence in your courage, devotion to duty, and skill in battle. We march in our might to complete victory. May God's blessing rest upon each of you on this Christmas Day.

G. S. PATTON, JR.,
Lieutenant General
Commanding, Third United States Army

PRAYER

Almighty and most merciful Father, we humbly beseech Thee, of Thy great goodness, to restrain these immoderate rains with which we have had to contend. Grant us fair weather for Battle. Graciously hearken to us as soldiers who call upon Thee that armed with Thy power, we may advance from victory to victory, and crush the oppression and wickedness of our enemies, and establish Thy justice among men and nations. Amen.

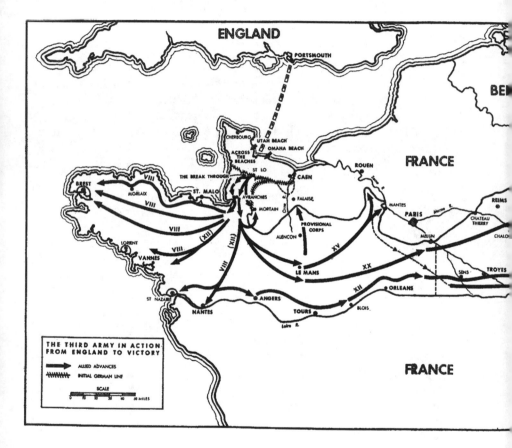

THE THIRD ARMY IN ACTION
FROM ENGLAND TO VICTORY

→ ALLIED ADVANCES
⋙ INITIAL GERMAN LINE

SCALE
0 10 20 30 40 50 MILES

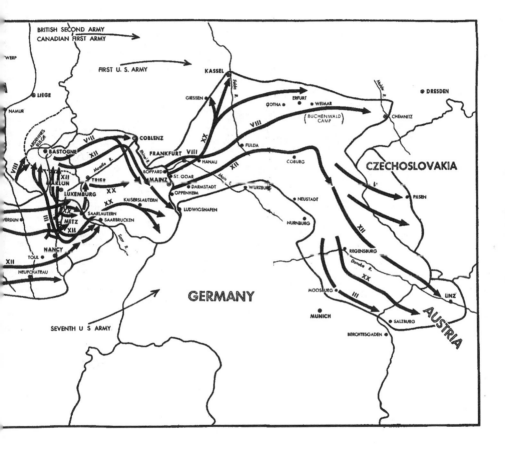